The Wisdom of
OLD DOGS

LESSONS IN LIFE,
LOVE AND FRIENDSHIP

The Wisdom of
OLD DOGS

LESSONS IN LIFE, LOVE AND FRIENDSHIP

ELLI H. RADINGER

TRANSLATED BY GEORGE ROBARTS

MB

MIRROR BOOKS

First published by Mirror Books in 2019
This edition published in 2020

Mirror Books is part of Reach plc
10 Lower Thames Street
London EC3R 6EN

www.mirrorbooks.co.uk

© Elli H. Radinger 2018
English translation by George Robarts

The rights of Elli H. Radinger to be identified as the author
of this book have been asserted, in accordance with the
Copyright, Designs and Patents Act 1988.

Originally published in Germany as *Die Weisheit alter Hunde: Gelassen sein,
erkennen, was wirklich zählt – Was wir von grauen Schnauzen über das
Leben lernen können* © 2018 by Ludwig Verlag, a division of Verlagsgruppe
Random House GmbH, München, Germany.

ISBN 978-1-912624-90-4

Typeset by Danny Lyle

Printed and bound in Great Britain by
CPI Group (UK) Ltd, Croydon, CR0 4YY

A CIP catalogue record for this book is available from the British Library.

Every effort has been made to fulfil requirements with regard to
reproducing copyright material. The author and publisher will be
glad to rectify any omissions at the earliest opportunity.

1 3 5 7 9 10 8 6 4 2

Cover images: iStockphoto

"Lord, help me be
the person my
dog thinks I am."

Contents

Introduction

The changes happened little by little. Right under my nose, and yet out of my sight. Every day she got a tiny bit older, a millionth more mature. It escaped my notice. Then, all at once, she left me speechless. A squirrel just raced up a tree right in front of her. But instead of going after the little scamp as usual, barking indignantly and dancing round the tree, she stayed lying down and looked wistfully after the creature.

Astonished, I looked at her − and spotted the grey whiskers framing her muzzle. And her eyes, which all of a sudden looked a little foggy. My dog, Shira, was getting old. How could I have missed it? I had seen it without noticing it. I hadn't taken a step back.

Parents of grown-up children often speak of the fright they get when leafing through the family album. They see the pictures of their little ones, playing on the beach and splashing about in armbands in the pool, and they ask themselves: What happened? Where along the way between childhood, teenagehood and adulthood did we lose them? How come we didn't notice they were getting older?

I recently looked at Shira's baby photos: a podgy, nearly-white labrador puppy, sticking her head through the spokes of the steering wheel in my car. Encounters with canine companions. First attempts at swimming, on a long lead, just to be on the safe side. Fetching a toy bigger than she was. On a walk half a year later, a teenager now, gangly and awkward, still yet to grow into her paws.

When I first held this wriggly fur ball in my arms, it didn't cross my mind that her growing old would be so difficult for me. After the exhausting puppy years and her difficult adolescence, I relaxed into her adulthood and looked forward to our "retirement" together. My vision: Shira would sleep all day and I'd write in peace. She'd be content to lie there by my side, and wouldn't need a packed programme. I'd have less work to do. How wrong I was. An old dog creates a good deal of work, and demands a lot of patience and extra-special care.

Old age can be a challenge for animals and their human companions. But it can also be an opportunity for us to get to know and love new sides to them. We adapt more readily to their needs. This is our chance to give back some of the unconditional love, patience and tolerance that they have shown us throughout their lives.

Introduction

I look down at my dog, who is lying under my desk. She senses that I am looking at her, but doesn't get up. Instead, her tail begins to beat against the floor. Thud, thud, thud. We are brought together by this noise. I kneel down beside her and take her head in my hands. Her floppy ears slip like velvet through my fingers. I trace my fingertips over her body, feeling the nodes of fat here and there. Shira is still an attractive, slim dog, with glossy blonde fur.

I bow my head and kiss her gently on the soft part of her muzzle under her eye. For a precious few seconds, neither of us stirs. We hold on to this magical moment. Then I get up and turn my attention back to my work. Shira lets out a long snuffling breath and goes back to sleep.

Moments like this, when I feel my close bond with my dog, take on particular significance now. I have always been glad to have her in my life, but I am more aware than ever of the finite nature of our relationship, and that makes me value her presence even more.

Shira is 13 years old. In human years (about 93) she has long since overtaken me. When she's trotting around outside with a spring in her step, burying her snout in the grass, or running riot with her doggy pals, her age isn't at all obvious. "She's still young, right?" Other dog owners frequently ask me that. It's only noticeable in the evenings following a long walk, as she slips off the sofa slowly and tentatively, to ease the strain on her weary bones. And she has to make more effort to get up out of her favourite big armchair. On our walks, she lies down more frequently if I stop moving. That's right, I have to take the occasional breather nowadays too.

I have been keeping a diary about Shira's life, as I want to preserve every moment in the hope that it will help me to cope better with the pain of loss – which will inescapably come.

I know what's in store for me. I've already shared my life with two other dogs, until they died of old age, and I stayed by their side all the way. Now the time has come to prepare myself once more – as far as that's ever possible. Essentially, this is my story too. I am witnessing a creature I love more than anything else growing old and beginning her journey towards death. I'm the one who at some point will have to make the yes-or-no decision. I must learn to deal with change and accept the inevitable. One day I will take Shira's life in my hands, and I will have to decide what to do with it. And that frightens me.

While writing this diary, I have discovered not only that I am preparing myself for my dog's old age and eventual passing, but that this is also an opportunity to look back on our life together – on a relationship that has become richer and more intimate with every passing year. Over the last few years we have both aged, and we have experienced the same things. That is often the case when you've lived with dogs for a long time. Shira and I have learned what there is to learn in this life. We know the rules and we have made peace with the world. We are enjoying our time together.

Introduction

The most difficult chapters of this book for me to write were the ones about saying goodbye to our beloved pets. For a while, dear readers, I even wondered whether I should trouble you with them at all. My publishers sounded a note of caution. But since this is a personal book, I decided to lay bare the whole spectrum of feelings that life with an old dog has to offer. How could I write about the wisdom of old dogs without mentioning the most profound wisdom, the most valuable lesson they have to share with us? Because ultimately, the way they negotiate their final months is their greatest gift of all.

Dogs enrich our lives. The older they get, the more precious the time we are able to spend with them becomes. Living with an old dog, helping them through their final years, opens our eyes and hearts. We discover that old age and death can teach us a great deal, and that being prepared for death also means being prepared for life.

Age: A Question
of Perspective

In his Theory of Relativity, Albert Einstein explained the concept of time with the famous "twin paradox". One twin flies into space in a rocket, while the other one stays on Earth. After a certain length of time, the astronaut flies back to Earth at the same speed. On arrival, they both realise that the twin who stayed on Earth is noticeably older than the twin from outer space. According to Einstein this is logical, because rapid movement through space means that time has "slowed down" for the astronaut.[1] In other words, how quickly or slowly time passes depends on how fast you're moving.

I don't need a rocket to see time flying. My dog is enough. I got Shira when she was an eight-week-old puppy. Today – at 13 – she is older than me. I look at her and ask her, "How on earth have you got so old?"

Shira's in a good mood and throws me a cheeky look that says, "You're one to talk."

And of course, she's right. I've aged as well. I don't know how Shira feels about getting older – I'd like to think she just accepts it and perhaps even enjoys it.

Right now, she's lying under my desk, her back to the radiator. Now and then she stretches her legs out like a cat, digs her claws into the carpet, and looks up at me. Then she takes a deep, noisy breath and goes back to sleep. One forepaw over the other, as if in doggy prayer, she twitches gently.

Ageing is uncharted territory for each and every one of us, despite the fact that humans have been doing it since time immemorial. But it shouldn't be a daunting prospect to spend the last years of our lives sleeping next to someone we love, dreaming of what has been and what could yet be.

Shira was a sweet little puppy dog who used to romp through the meadows with her floppy ears flying about all over the place. She'd stumble over her oversized paws and snowball through the grass, only to pick herself straight back up again to chase after a startled butterfly. She'd be gone in a flash. After the puppy years came puberty and her rebellious phase, followed by year after wonderful year with my grown-up dog.

And then came the day I realised that my once comical bundle of fur had become an old-timer, who preferred cosying up on the sofa to running after tennis balls, and whose limbs creaked when she stood up. To all intents and purposes, I was going the same way. The only difference between us was that Shira had aged on fast-forward.

One friend of mine still refuses to be called "old" at the age of 70. Another was given a "cruise for the elderly" by her children as a 75th birthday present, but wouldn't accept the gift because she didn't think of herself as an "old person".

I have looked forward to old age all my life: for me, it's always represented freedom from social constraints and expectations. I'd finally be able to do everything I wanted, and people would smile placidly and say, "Look at that mad old lady."

I celebrated the arrival of the menopause with a "Red Hot Mamas" party. The only guests I invited were menopausal women. We all wore red, and I served spicy food like chilli con carne and Thai curries.

Today I am 67, and my chances of reaching the big 100 are statistically good. Naturally I haven't been spared the aches and pains of ageing, no more than Shira has. But from her example I am learning how to age positively and how to make the best of it.

According to the Bible, the oldest person who ever lived was Methuselah, who reached a cool 969 years old (his son

Lamech only made it to 187).[2] The Australian Cattle Dog Bluey was, according to the *Guinness Book of Records*, the oldest dog in the world, living to 29 years and five months. Maggie the Kelpie, also from Australia, set a new record in 2016.[3] She was 30 years old, although she was not officially recorded as the oldest dog in the world, because her owner, the farmer Brian McLaren, lost her birth certificate and the accompanying paperwork. As a result, her exact age couldn't be determined. But when McLaren got Maggie as an eight-week-old puppy, his son Liam had just turned four. Today Liam is 34.

When I tried to use an online tool to calculate Maggie's age in human years, I was denied: *Please enter a number under 25*. Evidently the programmers assumed dogs never made it beyond 25. Maggie's age equates to around 200 human years.

The respective life expectancies of humans and dogs have risen continuously over the decades, and are still rising today. For dogs, it has gone up by three years within the last 20 years. This is thanks to better medical provisions and more species-appropriate nutrition and care.

Most dogs reach between eight and 15 years of age. Only very rarely do they make it as far as 20. Researchers at the University of Göttingen collected data from more than 50,000 dogs of 74 different breeds, and established that larger dogs die sooner than smaller ones.[4] And pedigree dogs consistently die earlier than mongrels. The bulldog, which on average does not make it past six, has the lowest life expectancy of any breed.

The study's conclusions should unsettle me: as a labrador, Shira belongs to one of the larger breeds. I can, however, count her a mongrel, because her father was a labrador and her mother was a flat-coated retriever. So I've bought a bit of time there. I breathe out. Got away with it this time. I know the feeling of living in latent danger. While I was researching wolves in America's Yellowstone National Park, I spent every day in an area that sits only about five kilometres above an enormous chamber of blistering magma. There, a "supervolcano" could erupt at any time. Scientists expect an eruption every 600,000 years. The most recent was 640,000 years ago, so a large-scale eruption is overdue.

Undaunted, I tell myself that it won't happen yet. That sort of thing doesn't happen to *me*. It won't happen now.

It's the same with Shira. 13 years old? That's nothing. It goes without saying that I want her to stay healthy and live as long as possible.

So, is there a magic formula for living a long life? I tried to find out, asking dog owners who read my online newsletter to describe life with their pets. I received over 200 responses, and would like to thank each and every person who told me their story and opened their heart to me. Their anecdotes moved me deeply and brought me to tears often enough. First and foremost, though, their letters gave me hope.

Take, for example, Kathy's dog Peggi. The 18-year-old cross-breed of Tibet terrier and cocker spaniel spends most of her time with Kathy's 78-year-old mother in Hamburg. These two old girls have sought and found one another – and both are still fighting fit. Or there's Heike's Malta, a street dog who lived to 16. Pocolino, Rosemarie's dog, came from Fuerteventura and reached the ripe old age of 20. Filou, Andrea's terrier crossbreed, is 19. Many of my readers' dogs reached (or are) 15, 16, or even older. By comparison, Shira is still a young buck, which gives me hope that 13 isn't so elderly after all.

But did I find a magic formula? Sadly, I'm going to have to disappoint you. There's no secret recipe for a long life – for dogs or humans. Today, the issues that make dogs "age" prematurely are the same as the ones that affect us: poor diet, obesity, lack of exercise, and insufficient mental stimulation.

Nonetheless, you can do everything "right" or everything "wrong" – it is ultimately meaningless. Nothing can absolutely guarantee that Fido (or you) will live longer. There are endless studies telling us humans how to live, what to eat, and which sports to play in order to reach 100. But you could still leave the house tomorrow and be hit by a bus. So what really counts is the quality, not the quantity, of our time on Earth.

So I decide not to keep driving myself mad. Age isn't an illness, for people or their pets. Shira, according to my online calculator, is 93 in human years, taking into account her weight of 25kg. She has overtaken even my 87-year-old mother.

Age: A Question of Perspective

I pause to take stock. How has Shira changed in her old age? When she is asleep under my desk as she is now, she radiates perfect calm. In my eyes, she is eternally young. We have been doing everything together for years: lengthy walks, lake-swimming, fetching balls (okay, I've done less of that than Shira). Sometimes I long for her to be young again, but mostly I am enjoying our time together now more than ever. Our mutual understanding grows deeper every day: we trust each other blindly, and we know what the other one wants. When I look at her, I know what she's thinking. We have a well-functioning daily routine.

But the signs of her age can no longer be ignored. Her golden fur has thinned and greyed in many places. She is losing more and more underfur. To compensate, she wears a fleece in winter and a raincoat when it's drizzling. She gets cold more quickly.

Her once-dark nose has turned light brown. Little warts and sties have started to emerge here and there, as they did recently in the inner corners of her eyes before disappearing again a few weeks later. Several fatty lumps have appeared beneath her fur. I took her for a check-up, where they were diagnosed as benign tumours (lipomas) growing around her ribcage.

Shira's eyesight is also going. Her warm brown eyes look increasingly bluish and foggy, and she's less sure of herself in the dark.

But her vision evidently does not have as important a part to play in her life as her other senses. Dogs have a substantially keener sense of hearing than us: they can detect sounds from four times further away than we can. Shira's hearing, though, has been in decline for months now. Initially she just had selective hearing, but not anymore. How is she coming to terms with that? When I stand near her and call her name, she doesn't react. Usually I have to touch her gently to get her attention. At least she hasn't lost her sense of touch. She detects vibrations in the floor and "hears" me when I stamp my feet.

In fact, her deafness has its advantages: our New Year this time round was a relaxing one, for the first time ever. The things I used to do to try to calm down my frightened dog on New Year's Eve or during thunderstorms – from special pheromone collars to homeopathic soothing drops, to noise conditioning. Nothing helped. Two years ago I even spent New Year in a wickedly expensive and completely isolated luxury hotel. Peak prices, minimum stay four nights! And still I had to calm down my trembling dog when the first fireworks went off far away in the city centre. I reject the notion that you should ignore an anxious pet, "to avoid validating its fear". I see it as my responsibility not to desert Shira at moments like that. So I hold her in my arms to make her feel safe. I don't care if I "should" do that or not. I just do it – because it makes me feel better too.

And now my dog is deaf. It can be exasperating when we go out for a walk and she can't hear me calling her, but in other situations it's a blessing. Despite the firecrackers and fireworks in our neighbourhood, New Year's Eve this year left her totally unfazed. The limitations of old age can also have their advantages.

Nonetheless, I have to be more alert when we go out for walkies these days. On one occasion, Shira suddenly vanished in the woods. She just snuffled off into the undergrowth and disappeared. I called and called after her – no response. Obviously. I clapped my hands and eventually resorted to my dog whistle, blowing it again and again until my own eardrums couldn't take it anymore. Still nothing. I started to panic, took a step back – and almost stumbled right over her. She had been standing behind me the whole time, giving me a quizzical look. "Hello, I'm right here. What's all the fuss about?" My relief was immeasurable.

Since Shira was a puppy, I've been teaching her visual signals, combining verbal cues with a gesture. She responds to "Come here", "Sit", "Down", and "Stay" – as long as I can get her to look at me. But that, too, is less of a problem in her old age, because Shira has become very dependent and is constantly looking round to check I'm still there. In areas she doesn't know, I keep her on a long lead or a Flexi lead to be on the safe side.

Contact seems to have become more important for her. She loves being stroked, and actively seeks out physical contact, which of course I enjoy too. It takes longer for her to wake up from a deep sleep, and when she does she sometimes seems to have forgotten where she is. When she goes for a final turn in the garden in the evenings, she occasionally stops and just stands there, staring into space. What's she thinking at those moments? Wearily, I go over to her in my pyjamas and lead her back into the house.

Recently she came down to the cellar with me and didn't follow me back up. I went to look for her and found her in my workshop. She was just standing there, looking up at me, happy to see me. It was as if she didn't know where she was anymore. Is that the first sign of dementia? My other dogs didn't have it. Or has that only occurred to me now because dementia and Alzheimer's in dogs are more topical, and we know more about them thanks to the internet and various other sources? I escorted my disorientated senior citizen back up the stairs. That's just the way it is – we need to look out for each other more these days.

Shira's energy levels change with the weather. On chilly, dry days, as on warm ones, she lollops through the fields like a young pup. But cold, wet weather rankles her. On those days, she prefers to stay in her basket.

Shira still gets excited when I pick up her dummy, which she first learned to fetch as a little puppy. Made from robust cotton, it looks a bit like a long pencil case, only it isn't filled with stationery, but with artificial pellets or some other waterproof material. The dummy is designed in the shape of a game bird, attached to a throwing rope that I can use to launch it a long way. Like most labradors, Shira loves retrieving it – it's in her genes. She skips impatiently around me as she waits for me to throw it. And she absolutely adores swimming out after it at every opportunity she gets.

Lately even her voice has changed. Her bark, previously sonorous and deep, has morphed into a jarring note, high and shrill like an opera diva who's lost her voice.

She needs more time nowadays to adapt to new situations and to get to grips with new tasks. I find it even more important to keep giving her new mental challenges, such as tracking scents. Even if she now takes much longer to pick up a scent, she's no less proud of herself when she finds the object I've hidden.

But Shira is becoming more anxious and less sure of herself on many fronts. In this regard, I try to give her as much support as possible. For example, I am particularly careful when she meets other dogs, and make sure that she only comes into contact with good-natured ones. Fierce, strong dogs could injure her at play if they jumped on her. My old girl's wellbeing is my number one priority, and the phrase "They'll sort it out between themselves" is one I find even more intolerable now than ever before.

Unfortunately, there's no secret of eternal youth for dogs either. The ailments of old age that Shira suffers from are the same ones that every elderly person knows all too well. I'm glad that I'm now a "Golden Ager" like my dog. If I were still young I'd have more difficulty seeing things from her perspective. My two previous dogs reached 15 and 16 years old, and if I had known then what I know now, I could perhaps have made them happier and made their final years easier.

We all want to stay fit for as long as possible. For dogs it's the same as for people: exercise and a good diet keep you healthy in the long term. As far as nutrition is concerned, I've stopped experimenting with Shira. Since every past attempt at changing her diet has resulted in diarrhoea or flatulence, I'm sticking to her tried-and-tested food formula. That way it's less stress for both of us. She gets a dog biscuit in the morning, special canned food for old dogs at noon, and a handful of dry food in the evenings. If a particular diet is working well and the dog is healthy, there's no need to change it. We humans know just as well what we can stomach and what we can't.

I know of some groups in the canine community who promote their food regimes as the "right" ones for dogs, and I'm aware of the war of opinions being fought out in internet forums on this issue. But instead of wasting my precious time searching for the "perfect" food, it's more important for me just to spend quality time with my dog.

The fact is that dogs (and humans) who are thinner and consume fewer calories live longer. With every extra kilo, we shorten our life expectancy. Shira's joints are helped enormously by the fact she is a dainty dog – which is unusual for a labrador.

My old girl and I both go to physiotherapists. No, not the same one. I get my back pain massaged away, while Shira gets laser acupuncture for her back and her joints. I also do exercises with her most days to keep her moving. She slaloms through my legs, does 360-degree turns on command – "twist" to turn to the right, "circle" to the left – and can never go quickly enough from sitting to lying down. Shira will happily play the circus dog for a biscuit.

Alongside regular visits to the vet, I've been taking her for a "geriatric health check" every six months since she was 11. Designed specifically for old dogs, this check-up is intended to catch early on any changes in the musculoskeletal system, the sensory organs, the cardiovascular system, and the internal organs. This unfailingly falls victim to my friends' laughter or ridicule. They think a geriatric health check for a dog is beyond barmy. I think it's sensible, as it lets me know how healthy my dog really is.

I'm very lucky to have a dream team of vets: specialists in traditional veterinary medicine, homeopathy, and physio-therapy. This combination of brilliant women, all at one clinic, is a huge gift for which I am thankful. Every dog owner must find the vet that suits them and their dog. I spent a long time looking, tried several out, and now finally feel we are in good hands.

One common problem with old dogs is dental calculus. Since Shira had to have major surgery to remove four teeth, I've taken more care to ensure that her calculus is less bad, and try to clean her teeth fairly regularly. She doesn't have much time for that, but I've discovered that she does like chicken-flavoured toothpaste – a tasty snack.

I have tried everything the old-dog market has to offer. To help Shira get into my car, I've tested out several different ramps, and chosen a collapsible aluminium one from a Swiss company that enables Shira to get up and down safely and without any problems.

At the first signs of old age I started to adapt Shira's surroundings, and couldn't help noticing with a smile that the changes I made weren't only making life easier for her, but for me as well.

As my old bathroom needed to be renovated, I rebuilt a new accessible one with a ground-floor shower – more suitable for elderly people. "Already?" a friend asked me. Yes – if not now, when? Anything I can do now saves me having to do it later.

Because Shira has problems climbing the stairs, I've moved my bedroom from the first floor to the ground floor. It now opens straight out onto the garden. My house has gradually turned into a big cuddly kennel for my four-legged old lady. In every room there are orthopaedic dog beds that fit her body shape and take the pressure off her joints. I'm getting jealous of her now, and have resolved to get myself a similar mattress.

But Shira still prefers the sofa most of the time, even if she has to make the laborious jump up onto it. Non-skid carpets make it easier for her to walk over the smooth plank flooring.

Yes, an old dog is hard work. Back when she was a puppy I had to wipe away little accidents or replace chewed-up cushions. Some time in the future I will have to deal with a couple more mishaps, but at least Shira won't chew up the furniture with the few teeth she has left.

This morning I woke up early as always and wrote for two hours. Shira lay asleep by the radiator. Then she woke up and stretched.

"So, do you want to go out?" I opened the door to the garden. It was pouring. Too wet for my lady labrador, who in any other circumstances can't get enough of water. She turned round and decided to snooze for a bit longer. On nicer days, when the sun is shining and she's overslept, her head shoots up when I push my desk chair back, and she goggles at me, wide-eyed.

"How about it, shall we go for a spin?"

"Yes! Yes! Yesssss! I thought you'd never ask."

Daily strolls are far more than just an everyday necessity for us. They are opportunities for us to relish our life together and the natural world around us. For me, every walk is a kind of sacred time. An interesting study by Dr Thomas Fletcher and Dr Louise Platt, entitled "(Just) a walk with the dog? Animal geographies and negotiating walking spaces"[5] suggests that a dog walk isn't "just" a walk, but much more: going out with the dog is a "highly sensory and complex activity" as well as "a potentially important cultural space in which to understand relationships between humans and dogs". According to Fletcher and Platt, the personalities of both dog and dog owner become clearly visible on a walk together. This is where the balance of power between dogs and humans comes to the fore. The state of the dog lead speaks volumes about their relationship: a slack lead suggests harmony, a taut lead suggests contradictory ideas about who's in charge.

As part of their research, Fletcher and Platt went round the north of England interviewing people who regularly walked their dog. Most interviewees considered walks to be crucial for the health and wellbeing of their dog. They didn't just think of it as a responsible dog owner's "duty", but felt it was above all about making their dog happy.

Dog owner Jane said of her walks with Copper, her Afghan hound, "The best thing of all is seeing Copper running through a field. I once measured how fast he was going: he can hit 30mph. You could mistake him for a leopard. When I see him running, when he's so in his element, I realise how happy that makes me."

Shira, of course, can't get near that sort of speed – our fitness programme has its limits. Usually she's lagging behind me by the end of a long walk. But sometimes she turns on the gas, snapping off a stick that she absolutely has to take with her. She runs off with it, tosses it up in the air, lets it fall and rolls about on top of it, kicking her legs in the air. At the end of those days she needs extra time to recuperate. Usually that means tomorrow will be a rest day with only short strolls.

Our life together has taken on new dimensions. In our daily human lives, the tempo is often very high, and there's no time left to discover the little things in life. But Shira persuades me to keep pausing to enjoy the moment.

My life with my old dog is now significantly quieter than it was when she was a puppy. She is grown up now, and one look is enough for us to understand one another. Shira is remarkably undemanding, and is happy just to be around me. In return, I make sure I cater for her needs and take things at the speed she wants.

Sometimes, when she is really dawdling and our walk is turning into more of a standstill, as she wants to have a good sniff at every blade of grass, I am tempted to drag her along behind me. "Come on, I haven't got all day." But then I become aware of the fact that one day in the not-too-distant future I will wish I could watch her dawdling like that just one more time. I am learning to keep my haste in check and take our walks at a leisurely pace. And I find that this also helps me find peace.

Dogs' lives are so tightly interwoven with our own. When we get them as puppies, they're sweet and magical – and they drive us to desperation, chewing up shoes or furniture and generally causing chaos around the house. Then we teach them to behave, which sometimes actually works. Our relationship deepens over the course of time. And as our dogs age, the tides turn, and we're the ones that begin to learn – to relax, to have fun, and to enjoy the simple things in life. Life is undeniably better with a dog at your side.

Our old dogs have gathered a lot of experience – with cars, children, strangers, neighbours, vets, other dogs and cats, and hunting wild animals. And they have weighed up every experience in their dog lives according to two simple criteria: is it good for me or is it not good for me?

As a dog owner, I don't have to be on my guard all the time anymore, because over the years, my dog has got smarter. Shira used to love chasing rabbits, though she wasn't allowed to. Today she's allowed to, but she doesn't stand a chance of catching them. Sometimes, when a bunny hops out right in front of her on a walk, she looks in the opposite direction – deliberately, as if she actively wants to take her eyes off the prize. Rabbits don't interest her anymore. Older dogs assess their chances with precision. It is their own experience – not their training – that elicits this exemplary behaviour. And now that my old girl has accumulated a practically inexhaustible wealth of experience, she has become my absolute dream dog. When she was still an exhausting, obstinate young pup, I looked forward to this part of her life. When we gaze at each other today, as kindred spirits, I see myself reflected in her foggy eyes. Yes, my dog is old – so what? She senses the changes in herself and adapts to them, without making an ideological spectacle of it. Old age is a more interesting and significant part of our lives than we realise. And it is the time when we dog owners reap the fruits of what we have sown over the course of a lifetime. So let's look forward to it.

Look After
Your Pack

My friend Bob is an author and first-time dog owner. He was recently invited to a fellow author's book launch and the cocktail party afterwards. The other writers had plenty to talk about: Bob listened patiently as one woman told him all about her next book deal. Eventually, he muscled in with his own exciting news. On a research trip to Spain, he'd been approached by a dog who he'd taken back home with him.

"I was so excited to tell her about it, I just couldn't stop talking," Bob told me afterwards. "I just went on and on about how wonderful the dog is and how lucky I was to be able to adopt him."

The woman listened for a while before asking, "But you don't hug and kiss him, right?"

She was convinced he would reply in the negative.

"Yes, of course I do. All the time!" my friend replied, his whole face lighting up.

At that, the woman slipped back into the crowd to find someone else to talk to.

Only a few months ago, Bob would have been on her side. Dogs and dog people hardly interested him at all. He couldn't understand what they found so amazing about their pets. Then, one day on a beach in Malaga, he met Amigo, a scruffy, skinny mongrel with a grey muzzle, and it hit him.

"He looked a little bit like me," he grins, pointing at his trimmed salt-and-pepper beard. "Amigo decided he was mine, just like that. He followed me everywhere. There was no way I could have left him behind."

The stray introduced Bob to a whole new world. He met people he would never otherwise have got to know – on walks in the park or trips to the woods. Suddenly he, a reclusive lone wolf, had a vast extended family (24% of the UK adult population owns a dog).[6]

When we decide to live with a dog, we are committing to a lifelong process of translation. We do our best to understand our dogs, and vice versa. But our language begins to resemble that of adults talking to babies – silly, nonsensical, and incomprehensible to anyone but ourselves. The names I call Shira are things like "Waggly-Tail", "Fairy", "Sugar Mouse". Do they mean anything to her? Presumably she barely gives it a second thought. I could just as well call her "Hoover" or "Einstein". It's my inflection and expression that matter, that make her wag her tail with glee when I talk to her. I'd love to know what names she has for me. "Desk Dumpling"? There's so much that I don't know and will never find out.

Dogs lead us into a world that differs greatly from our own, a place that completely transforms us. Fall in love with a dog and you enter a whole new sphere, a universe where there are rules, bonds, and rituals that you never knew about before.

Everything changes – sometimes very subtly, sometimes dramatically. Your walks get slower. You no longer hurry to a specific destination, but amble through the streets, because your dog has to stop to snuffle around every tree and every lamppost. Your clothes belong to the dog now. Forget your smart suit – clunky walking boots, an old anorak, a thick sweatshirt, and the road-worker look is complete. Even the way you speak changes. It's not the words you use that matter, it's your tone of voice. You speak in a high-pitched baby voice to a puppy, but adopt a deep, soothing tone to address an older dog. Your home transforms itself to accommodate your pet. At night you wake the whole house up by treading on a squeaky toy, and your cupboards are rammed full with dog food, flea shampoo and poo bags. Your conversations change, too. Relaxed dinners with friends begin to revolve around food intolerances, bowel movements, deworming and flea treatment. As you whip your phone out to show everyone your latest photos, don't be surprised when non-dog-owners suddenly remember an "important thing" that they have to get back home for – if they're not already gone by that point. You turn down romantic weekends away because dogs aren't allowed. And your former friends start to suggest meeting up at pizzerias instead of coming to yours, because they know they'll never get the dog hair out of their clothes again. The phrase "Don't be like that, it's just a dog" gets your hackles up, and anyone who says that to you is putting your friendship on the line.

Undoubtedly you are part of this mad, loveable family, otherwise you wouldn't be reading this book. Your dog's so important that you'd do anything for it, wouldn't you? And sometimes you go a bit overboard, don't you?

Dogs are our families, partners, friends, and – that's right – even our children. They are pack animals, just like wolves. You only find lone wolves in fairy tales or in bad films. And we humans are the same: we aren't loners, we're social animals who are dependent on others and need to feel part of a group. For our four-legged friends, family – that's us – is the most important thing. That's why dogs stay with their human family even if they're treated badly by them. The wellbeing of the group is more important than anything else. Later in this book we will see the lengths people go to in order to provide for their furry family members.

I've spent my whole life around dogs, from Axel, my grandfather's alsatian, to several boarding dogs we took in. They are a natural part of my life. If we grow up around animals, we form an intrinsic, primal bond with them. The phrase "I grew up with dogs" suggests a longing for the purity and innocence of childhood, revealing our desire to return to simpler times and less complicated relationships.

When I'm working on a book, I keep changing where I sit to write, to prevent back pain. I write at my desk, at the kitchen table, in the garden, standing up.

Shira lies at my side the whole time. Whenever I get up to go somewhere else, she follows me. She wants to be close to me, just as members of a wolf pack like to lie close together. Some dogs need space. Shira isn't one of them. The closer she is to me, the happier she seems to be. As she curls up under my desk, she lets out a deep sigh of contentment. She knows that she belongs to me and can count on me, because I will always protect her. And I know that she's there for me. Shira is great at reading my moods. Her muzzle, which she rests on my knee when I'm not feeling good, makes all the difference.

Dogs stick with their pack, play with them, and defend them. Their needs are almost identical to ours: they want stable and rewarding relationships. Both humans and dogs love being looked after, and love caring for others. And dogs stand in solidarity with their humans. Sometimes we can't explain why a dog behaves differently towards different people. It often appears that they can identify a "bad" person and avoid contact with them.

Japanese scientists decided to test whether dogs have a sixth sense about people. Kazuo Fujita, Professor of Comparative Cognition at Kyoto University, led a team of researchers testing three groups of 18 dogs in role-play scenarios. The dogs were placed in two different situations. Both times, the protagonists of the scene were the dog's owner and two actors. In the first scene, the dog's owner is having difficulty opening a can of dog food. He asks one of his accomplices for help, while the other one isn't consulted. In this scenario, the dog accepts food from both strangers.

In the second scene, one of the actors refuses to help the owner opening the can, while the other one watches without intervening. The dog accepts food only from the neutral person and behaves standoffishly towards the person who didn't want to help its owner. This behaviour was observed in every dog.

"We proved for the first time that dogs make social and emotional evaluations of people, regardless of their own direct interests," says Fujita.[7] Dogs judge people by how they behave towards others – including other human beings. Perhaps we should take a leaf out of their book.

The mother of a friend of mine warned her to ask herself two questions when choosing a potential husband.

What's he like behind the wheel? And how does he behave towards his mother and other women? Good advice. Her winning candidate drives calmly and sensibly, and treats women, especially his mother, with politeness and respect.

THROUGH THICK AND THIN

It never fails to astonish me how few people plan ahead in case they die or become seriously ill. Last will and testament? We're still far too young for that. Medical directive? Later.

The family unit gives us safety and protection. If we bring a dog into our pack, we're making a promise to look after it. That's the foundation of our mutual trust. This promise holds through thick and thin – and even beyond the grave. We do occasionally think about what it'll be like when our dogs die, even if we don't like to imagine it. But hardly anyone thinks about what would happen to their four-legged friend if they were no longer able to look after it.

A conversation with a volunteer dog-walker at an animal shelter brought home to me what the consequences could be for Shira if I suddenly died or couldn't look after her anymore. The woman told me how difficult it is to rehome old dogs.

It happened in a flash. A momentary lapse in concentration, a squeal of brakes, and the clash of metal on metal cut through the winter air. None of the other passengers survived the accident. The only one who got lucky was Rotti, a 10-year-old rottweiler who was flung out of the car. The police took him to the vet, who treated his injuries, and then on to the animal shelter. No one from the victims' family wanted him. "We don't have time to look after our parents' old dog," they said.

In the shelter, they weren't holding out much hope. Dogs older than two, they said, only had a slim chance of finding a new home. Orphaned animals are often considered unadoptable because they are so downcast. They refuse to eat and take little interest in anything. They don't "sell themselves" well. It's even more difficult to rehome old or ill dogs, or "listed dogs" – breeds which are officially classified as dangerous, and which come with conditions attached to their behaviour. They are often referred to as "attack dogs". In some countries, rottweilers belong to this category.

After the trauma Rotti had experienced, he was now facing a gloomy, uncertain future. His physical injuries healed, but he was a lonely lost soul. He couldn't understand what had happened. Every day he waited patiently, hoping that his owners would come to collect him.

A kennel was found for him in the back row. In the runs next to him sat empty-eyed dogs who were also old or proving difficult to rehome. They had already given up hope. On visiting days, the noise was almost unbearable for Rotti. The young dogs and puppies in the front row barked, whimpered, whined, and jumped up behind the bars. They did everything they could to attract the visitors' attention. Word had got round that making a scene was the easiest way to conquer biped hearts.

Sometimes someone would go past Rotti's kennel and stop to look at the label affixed to the gate: "Rottweiler 'Rotti', 12 years old, neutered, no behavioural problems." They would study the dog, curled up in the far corner of his run, lying listlessly on a blanket, making no attempt to interact with the interested party. Rotti was grieving in silence. As day after day went by, he was overlooked again and again, and his precious life continued to go to waste.

In the neighbouring kennel lay a 15-year-old female cocker spaniel. Now and then she raised her head as a visitor went by, and looked at them through bleary eyes. 40 kilometres away, her former owner was sitting alone in an armchair in a care home, staring into space. He had dementia, and no longer remembered his furry companion of many years. Sometimes he sensed he was missing something – an ache, a distant longing – but he didn't know what it was.

Death is a touchy subject that very few people want to think about, but it is part of life – and, for dog owners, it is part of our duty of care to our pack. I absolutely do not want my dog to end up in an animal shelter one day. I must plan ahead.

Most people don't want to take this possibility into consideration, and don't want to make contingency plans. But we will all die one day, and some of us might get seriously ill or injured. What will happen to our animals then? Lack of planning could land them with strangers or consign them to an uncertain fate, and we wouldn't wish either of those things on them. With a bit of foresight and preparation, we can ensure there will be someone to care for them when we're no longer around.

I've made plans well in advance: for years I've had a will and a medical directive, which I check and update every two to three years. Good preparation saves me stress and prevents me making wrong decisions in an emergency. Once I'd put my own affairs in order, it was time to make contingency plans for my dog too.

Shira was given to me as a present by my friend Corina, who I affectionately call her "godmother". We've had a longstanding verbal agreement that she would look after my dog in an emergency. Shira loves her and enjoys spending time with her.

As always when I have pressing things on my mind, I talked it over with Shira first. After all, this was first and foremost about her.

I sat down next to her and spoke to her. "We need to talk." It's a sentence that every husband is afraid of. Shira, though, didn't roll her eyes. She kept her cool. She's used to it.

"So," I began, "this is serious, and it affects us both." That little word "serious" didn't seem to give my dog much cause for concern. She rolled over onto her back to let me tickle her stomach.

"Imagine something happened to me…"

"Eh?" Shira rolled back onto her side.

"That's right, I might have an accident and die suddenly. Then you'd be alone."

Now I'd got her attention. "What?"

"You never know when something like that could happen. If I wasn't there anymore, you'd be alone with no one to look after you."

"No one? But what about Grandma? Or the neighbours?"

"Let's assume they couldn't keep you for very long. Then you'd have to go to an animal shelter."

Shira's eyes widened. "An animal shelter? The things full of dogs in cages barking their heads off?" We once went to an animal shelter with a friend who wanted to adopt a dog.

"Yes, that's the one. Can you imagine that?"

"Nah!" Shira's clear and unmistakable response to every question she considers absurd and inconsequential.

"Okay, but in that case we need to work out where you could go in an emergency. Who would you want to stay with?"

"You."

"Right, but apart from me − where would you be happy? You're not the youngest anymore, you know. Old dogs don't get adopted very often. That could make life difficult for you."

Shira looked at me expectantly.

"What about going to Corina's?"

When Shira heard my friend's name, her tail started beating on the floor.

"Yes! Now? Let's go."

"No, not now. Some time in the future. Maybe." *Hopefully never,* I thought to myself.

That was that settled. I got up and went back to my desk.

If there's an emergency, it's vitally important to me that someone knows my dog needs to be looked after. Especially as I live on my own. If nobody knows I have a dog, she might have to sit tight in my flat for days, without food or water – a terrible thought.

A police officer told me about a poodle whose 32-year-old owner didn't come home one day. The man just vanished into thin air, and didn't reappear. The dog was alone at home for two weeks before a neighbour alerted the police, who retrieved the poor creature.

So I started making notecards.[8] In capital letters I wrote, "Important! In the event of an emergency, please notify the following people so that they can take care of my dog." Underneath I wrote the addresses and phone numbers of two people who said they'd be happy to look after Shira if something happened.

I put one of the cards in my wallet next to my driving licence, and another in the glove compartment of my car.

I went online and found reflective red "emergency pet stickers" where you can write in the number of pets you have, along with a contact number. I stuck one to my car window, and two more on the front and back doors of my house.

The next thing was to confirm in writing who would look after Shira in an emergency. I had several options: my parents, the neighbours, and Corina. Of course, I'd already talked to Shira's "emergency godparents" and amended my will to confirm who would "inherit" her.

While I was still working as a lawyer, one of my clients, a dog owner who was seriously ill with cancer, wanted to amend his will asking for his dogs to be put to sleep if he died. He was concerned for their welfare. "Better dead than in an animal shelter," he said. But we worked together to find a solution, in the shape of new "foster parents" for his dogs. This brought home to me just how important it is for dogs to get comfortable and build trust with people other than their owner. And the sooner the better. However difficult it might be for us to share a dog's love, it's in the animal's best interests.

So that all potential "godparents" would have the information they needed, I put together a "Dog" envelope that I attached to my will. It contains a copy of Shira's vaccination certificate, address and chip number, a list of the medications she takes on a regular basis, and information on her illnesses. I also added her favourite foods – as she's a labrador, that's "everything" – and which commands she responds to. I noted that Shira is deaf and responds to visual cues, and under "Other Particulars" I wrote, "Loves swimming."

It's never easy to think about your own death – and even harder to think about what will happen to the animals you leave behind. But now that everything was settled and I'd made provisions for my pack, I felt better. I don't ever want Shira to suffer because I didn't manage to get things sorted in time.

On our walks, I frequently bump into an old lady with a Zimmer frame and an alsatian crossbreed on a lead. The two of them walk extremely slowly. Once they're away from the road, the dog is allowed off the lead. I feel emotional when I see the two of them together. They seem so in tune with each other. One day I spoke to the lady. As I dug out treats from my jacket pocket and shared them out between our dogs, she told me the story of their unusual pairing. Her alsatian, Alba, is eight years old and suffers from severe arthritis. She takes tablets to ease the pain. The woman is 82. Her daughter got Alba from an animal shelter three years ago. But the daughter died suddenly not long afterwards. Knowing the dog was going to be returned to the shelter, the old lady intervened and decided to keep the creature. Since then, Alba has had a new owner. When the old lady isn't up to it, other family members walk the dog for her. Alba has adapted to her owner's pace and is a very friendly dog. They are the perfect couple. The two of them look out for each other. Alba got lucky, because many animal shelters don't let elderly people adopt – even if they're old dogs.

Adopting old rescue dogs is very rewarding, though, especially for older people who would prefer not to bring up an exhausting puppy. It's true that with an old dog your timeframe is limited, they're not as active, and veterinary bills are likely to be higher. But these dogs strike up a deep and intimate relationship with their humans, because they have been through dark times and have made it out the other side. They had given up hope of finding a new family, but now, given a new lease of life, they will relish every show of affection and every caress; they will appreciate sleeping in a comfy dog basket and having their own food and water bowls. It is a falsehood that old dogs can't learn and find it difficult to adapt to a new life. These dogs take their chances and spare no effort in winning their new family's approval. Anyone who has adopted an old dog knows that they are loving, even-tempered, and peaceful companions. They just don't get enough opportunities to show it.

Fortunately, there are now many more internet sites pairing up elderly humans and dogs, such as the "Oldies Club".[9]

When it comes to looking after your pack, another tricky subject is the unavoidable question of money. A dog can cost between £6,500 and £17,000[10] over the course of their lifetime.

Pet owners spare no expense to keep their animals healthy. A study by the University of Göttingen in Germany demonstrates just how much they spend: "In 2013, German vets made an annual turnover of around €2 billion just from treating pets. Medicine sales brought in another €500 million. Owners spent most on dogs, with cats in second place, followed by small animals, birds, and reptiles."[11]

The number of potential patients is huge, with an estimated nine million dogs in the UK alone.[12] If they get ill, the options include pills, drops and injections. According to the study, nearly 90% of dog owners take their pet to the vet at least once a year. Animals are the most important points of contact in many people's lives. We would give anything not to lose them. But caring for an old, ill dog can quickly become very expensive. A dog that has to have several operations can end up costing the same amount as a small car. Some owners are even forced to take out a loan.

Routine check-ups can cost £180 per year, which comes to £2,500 over a dog's lifetime. Research suggests that you should expect an average of five more significant health problems in a dog's life, coming to a cool £6,000. This seems like a reasonable estimate. Even if a dog doesn't need any operations, you might still have to deal with chronic conditions.[13]

When Shira had four molars removed last year, it cost £450. Fortunately she has been insured since she was a puppy, which covered the operation. In my view, having that kind of safety net is just part of the job of looking after a dog.

Finding out what really matters in life can be a painful experience. Sometimes money is tight and you can barely afford to feed your dog anymore. As a freelance author, I have reached a point on several occasions where I've had to decide between refuelling my car or buying food for my dog. It goes without saying that the car stayed firmly in the garage.

Homeless people are hit particularly hard, as their dogs are often all they have left. Lothar lives on the streets in a city centre with his old mongrel Lupo. Lupo is his whole world. He keeps his owner warm, protects him, and brings him happiness. Lothar proudly shows me his forearm, where he has a tattoo of Lupo's name and date of birth. When his dog was ill, Lothar was completely stumped: "I didn't have enough money for a vet. But I wanted to help him get better." Luckily, Lothar was assisted by his local authority, which provides free veterinary check-ups for pets belonging to people who are in financial need or living on the streets. The clinics are held by volunteer vets at a metro station. The cost of vaccinations and operations is covered by donations and sponsorship. Lothar is grateful that Lupo is well again. He shyly admits to me that he would even have been prepared to sell one of his kidneys on the black market just to help his furry friend. Fortunately, there was no need. Lothar and Lupo have nowhere to live and no money to spend, but they have each other. And ultimately that is all that matters.

Part of looking after our pack is having a partner we can rely on in difficult times. Now I know Shira's taken care of, I can concentrate fully on what I still hope will be a long life together.

See with
Your Heart

A bove my desk there's a photo of the Buckskin Gulch in Arizona, a 26km-long slot canyon in the southwest of the USA. The canyon is a popular subject for photos. The gulch's red sandstone walls, towering many metres high, are characterised by whirling curvatures formed over centuries by countless floods. With the right light and a dash of imagination, the rock formations begin to resemble all kinds of contorted figures and peculiar objects. In the foreground of the photo is a dog lying in the sand on the floor of the canyon. It's a red heeler, an Australian herding dog with short, red-flecked fur. What moves me about the picture is the fact that the dog is curled up in a thick, warm sleeping bag, fast asleep. That's what made me want to hang it up on my wall. Someone loved their dog so much that they tucked him in.

Jerry, a friend of mine from Arizona, saw the picture in a backpacker magazine. He tore it out and sent it to me. The photo instantly triggered something within me: a warm feeling of love and tenderness, and a sense of kinship.

I wanted to find out more about the photo's origins. After four weeks of thorough searching, I tracked down the photographer. Jesse Selwyn sent me the original and told me his story:

"This is Livy. She belongs to my brother and is a six-year-old boxer and heeler crossbreed. We got her from an animal shelter four years ago. She's a wonderful dog full of life and love, and she comes with us on lots of journeys, hikes and bike rides. My wife, my brother and I went on this hike in the first week of November 2016. Normally you can make it through the Buckskin Gulch in two days. On the first day we had to wade through countless waterholes and pools of varying sizes – we even had to swim through some of them. The water was ice-cold. At the end of the day, all of us – including Livy – were soaked through and freezing. Of course, we had brought dry clothes for ourselves, but we didn't have anything for Livy, who was shivering all over. So we wrapped her up in one of our sleeping bags. She warmed up quickly and fell asleep within a few minutes. This photo is a wonderful memory of our hike."

A sleeping dog, filthy and exhausted, nestled up in a downy sleeping bag. Whenever I look at the photo, it moves me. I feel connected to the dog's owner by an invisible bond. A bond of love, warmth and care, which we give our animals every day. A bond that makes us better people.

Saints are often depicted with halos round their heads. Dogs are born with invisible halos. When a dog enters a room full of people, it immediately attracts their attention (and makes them smile), and it stays that way as long as the dog is in the room. Even at a wedding.

Tom and Melinda were exchanging vows in church when their dog Boomer managed to wriggle in through the door and raced up to the altar to greet the couple, dancing around them and barking for joy. The whole congregation fell about laughing. The priest let the dog lie by its owners as he concluded the ceremony. Boomer accompanied them on their way out of the church, carrying a bouquet of flowers, surrounded by grinning friends and relations.

I can't imagine life without a dog. If I'm going away for work and can't take Shira with me, I leave her in the loving hands of my parents. She goes there for a nice, relaxing "spa holiday", but saying goodbye to her is still hard. I kiss her wet nose a thousand times and promise her, "I won't be long, I'll be home again soon!"

When we're apart, what do I do? I look out for dogs everywhere I go. The moment I see one with even the slightest resemblance to my labrador, I pounce on its unsuspecting owners. "Aaaaahhh... What a beautiful dog! Can I stroke him?" And straight away I'm on my knees, in ecstasy, as a dog I've never met before licks my glasses clean. I bury my head in its unfamiliar fur and look up at its owners with tears in my eyes. "Sorry. I just miss my dog so much."

Nods of understanding. Even if we don't speak the same language, the language of love and longing does the talking. I've often been at the other end of the lead, letting strangers stroke my dog. And Shira? All she understands is that someone's stroking her and telling her how wonderful she is. For an attention-seeking labrador like her, that's great news.

If I'm away from my dog, I see labradors *everywhere* – in city centres, in restaurants, in shops. If I turn enthusiastically to friends who don't have dogs, exclaiming, "Oh, how sweet! Did you see that dog back there?" I'm greeted with blank looks and shrugs. This manner of seeing with the heart has been coined "selective perception". My longing for my dog can sometimes be cured, or at least soothed, just by looking around me.

Granted, sometimes I'm only five minutes from home, at the supermarket on the corner, and still I can't stop myself crouching down to cuddle some old pooch waiting patiently for its owner outside the shop.

After book tours, when my parents and Shira come to collect me from the airport or the station, my dog is the only thing I see in the crowds of people. My gaze rests solely on her, on everything about her: she's sitting there, tense in concentration, looking up hopefully at passing travellers and snuffling at the air. No familiar scent just yet. Then she notices me, and suddenly there's no holding back. I fall to my knees as Shira leaps into my arms and covers my face with dog kisses. Pure joy. Smiling faces all around us.

Dogs radiate an inner light that makes people happy. Whether at airports, stations or city centres − we dog-lovers "recognise" each other. When I talk about dogs, the curtain of caution and self-consciousness that I often hide behind is torn down, and I put my trust in complete strangers because of the one thing that brings us together: dogs. We speak the same language and live in the same world, shaped by these delightfully loveable creatures. We are not alone.

As an author and wolf expert, I'm regularly invited to interviews and talk shows, usually with Shira. Lying at my feet as the rolling cameras fawn over her, she brings smiles to all the crew's faces. It's an old pearl of wisdom in the media industry: "Bring a dog with you, and it doesn't matter what you say. Everyone will just be looking at the dog."

It is a well-known fact that interacting with dogs sparks positive emotional reactions. They keep us healthy, in that

43

they slow our heartbeats down and lower our blood pressure, and they make us demonstrably happy, as levels of oxytocin (the so-called "love hormone") in our bloodstream rise when we stroke them.

We dog owners don't need science to prove this – we just know it. There are moments in our lives when our hearts open and we suddenly feel a deep and intimate connection with everything around us. Just like a moment I experienced recently in a city centre cafe.

I'm sitting in the cafe with three friends and five dogs in total. The dogs are lying calmly next to their owners, watching other humans passing by. Sometimes one of their tails begins to beat happily on the ground – who or what they've seen, we don't know.

Most people who see the dogs smile at them. Some come over and stroke them, children squat down next to them. Our table is right in the middle of a golden bubble of love. The fact I don't see any grumpy faces in the crowd of passers-by is probably due to my "selective perception".

Selective perception is the psychological phenomenon that makes us absorb certain aspects of our environment while excluding others.

Our visual world is a great big illusion. If you read the news over breakfast, either in print or on a tablet, would you be able to recall at noon what you read in the morning, besides the headlines? No? You looked without seeing. That happens to all of us several times a day, and it's known as "inattentional blindness". You only really notice things when you're making a conscious effort.

Everyone who drives knows this. You drive to work in the morning, and when you arrive you ask yourself how you got there so quickly. You've already forgotten what happened on the way.

While I was a student I went to a lecture on criminal law. In the middle of the session, the professor's secretary briefly came in to ask him to sign something. At the end of the lecture, the professor asked, "A little while ago my secretary brought something in for me to sign. Do you remember? Can you describe the woman?"

Silence. Most of us students had of course "seen" the woman, but we hadn't noticed her. Our descriptions were so different – tall, short, blonde, black-haired, some even thought the secretary was a man – that the exercise perfectly demonstrated how unreliable witness statements can be.

We humans only pay attention to what matters to us in the here and now. If you're hungry, you see restaurants and food everywhere you look. A pregnant woman will see an unusually large number of prams in a crowd, even though there are no more than usual. The brain filters information and shows us a world to match our own preoccupations – which is why dog owners see an overwhelming number of dogs. In the case of me and my old dog, it's grey muzzles that I see everywhere.

The Wisdom of Old Dogs

I take tai chi classes on warm summer evenings in the park. There's an old shaggy dog who regularly turns up there. He lies at the edge of the grass, watching us. Sometimes, if we all turn to him in sync or move towards him, he placidly wags his tail. He watches us with curiosity and concentration, radiating a positive energy that brings a smile to all our faces, even when we're hard at work.

When we're around dogs, we feel a spiritual connection to them. We speak the same language and understand them without speaking, bonding with them just by looking into their eyes and stroking their velvety fur. Animals teach us to live without words, to listen to other forms of consciousness, to readjust to new rhythms, and to see with our hearts.

Discover What
Really Matters

"You can't do that! You can't pack it all in just for your dog. What on earth is wrong with you?"

Well, what *was* wrong with me? I had just told my friends that I was shelving my research on wolves for the foreseeable future. For a quarter of a century I'd been flying to America several times a year to observe wild wolves in Yellowstone National Park. I had organised wolf tours, worked as a tourist guide in the park, written books about wolves, and delivered lectures and seminars on them. I'd met like-minded people and built my social circles around them. Wolves had enriched my life: personally, intellectually, and financially too. Now I was giving all of that up. Why? For my dog.

Over the last few years, every time I'd boarded that plane, I'd been a little more painfully aware that I didn't have much time left with Shira. I'd forgotten how much shorter her life was than mine.

When my friend Corina placed that bright, wriggly puppy in my arms in the summer of 2005, my world was suddenly reduced to Shira's size while simultaneously seeming to stretch out into an endless future. If everything went well, I had 15 happy dog years ahead of me.

Three years later I crafted Shira her own personal "Walk of Fame" in the basement of my house: I pressed her paw into a freshly poured slab of concrete and wrote the date 2008 underneath it. So much time still to come...

On holiday in South Tyrol in 2013, I got talking to some other tourists. A married couple were admiring my dog and stroking her. The woman asked me how old she was.

"Eight."

"What? Eight already? So she'll be dead soon?" her husband replied, with remarkable sensitivity. Their dogs had all lived to 10. I indignantly retorted that *my* dogs had all reached 15 or 16. But that still came as a shock – because at eight, Shira was already halfway there. Only eight more years!

At the end of every year I carry out a number of personal rituals, along with a review of the past twelve months. What was good about this year, what was bad? What did I do wrong and what am I thankful for? Then I update my diary and my address book, writing in new appointments and birthdays and removing the addresses of friends and acquaintances I'm no longer in contact with. In recent years I've had to remove more and more friends' addresses. They had died that year. I had planned to go and visit some of them. Too late.

In 2016, when I found Shira's upcoming birthday in my diary and wrote in "Shira 11", it hit me that our time together was increasingly finite, and that I didn't want to be away from her for long periods anymore. Something had to change. Suddenly it all became crystal clear. Things that used to be important didn't matter anymore. My priorities were different now. I wanted to spend Shira's final years with her; I wanted to be there for her just as she'd always been there for me. America and the wolves would still be there in five years' time, but Shira wouldn't.

My other dogs used to come with me to America. Klops, the first dog I owned, flew out with me to Vancouver, where we lived for three months in a camper van while I did my research. I met Lady in an American animal shelter. Before we flew back home to Germany, we spent half a year driving all round the USA. Shira, on the other hand, never boarded that plane with me. I don't want to force a transatlantic flight on her – she's too sensitive. Perhaps I've also become more anxious over the years.

In the USA, travelling with a dog is an arduous business. There are barely any hotels and only a few rental homes where dogs are allowed. Restaurants are a no-go, and in national parks, animals have to be kept on a lead and are only allowed to walk on the road – so no real freedom to roam around the backcountry.

While watching the wolves, or leading tour groups in Yellowstone, I wouldn't have been able to take my dog with me anyway. Some people on expensive long-haul trips aren't really on board with hairy travel companions. Shira had a better deal staying at home with my parents.

But now I didn't want to live without her anymore. My priorities had changed. The day came for my final flight to Montana, and I was packing my bags once more. Shira lay in her basket, eyeing me suspiciously. Nuzzled up in a light-coloured woollen blanket, she almost seemed to be merging into it. Her brown eyes followed my every movement. I stopped what I was doing and sat down next to her. I gently stroked her head. She closed her eyes with satisfaction.

"This is the last time," I promised her. "Really. The last time."

Mentally I was at home with Shira for the whole trip – ironic, really, because one of the main lessons I'd learned from wolves over the years was just how important it is to live in the here and now. But my longing for my dog was stronger than that. I woke up thinking about her, and was still thinking about her when I went to bed. When I saw the way the wolves greeted each other and played with each other, all I could think was: *just like Shira*. For the first time in many years, it was easy for me to say goodbye to Yellowstone. It wouldn't be for ever. Time wasn't important to me anymore – beyond its constant reminders for me to go home to Shira. How could a dog dominate my life like this? How could I restrict myself like this, even in the knowledge that I'd found real freedom?

I packed up everything I had in the USA, closed my American bank account, and cleared my research equipment out of the storage room. Then I said goodbye to my friends, promising to come back when my dog was no longer with me – hopefully not too soon, I silently prayed.

When I arrived at the airport with my heaps of excess baggage, my parents and Shira were waiting for me on the other side of customs. I sank to my knees and relished my dog's tumultuous greeting. All was well with the world again. I'd done the right thing.

Even if I still long for "my" wolves today, I've never regretted my decision for one moment. Shira and I have more time together now, and I'm learning to live my life one step at a time and to enjoy every moment. The time I spend with my dog now has become the most intense time of my life so far, in that I am not only receiving unconditional love every minute of every day, but am also constantly giving it back to her.

We dog-lovers all pay a price: falling in love with a creature whose life is so much shorter than ours.

I recently met a young married couple with a labrador puppy. My heart leapt. "Eight weeks," the man said proudly when I asked him how old the little one was. I stroked its soft puppy fur and gazed into its big eyes and little creased baby face. "Enjoy it while it lasts," I said. "It all goes far too quickly."

Did I really enjoy Shira's puppy years, or was I too busy trying to do everything right, trying to raise the perfect dog? Life with a puppy is so exciting – and tiring – that sometimes you don't get time to stop and marvel at this little living miracle.

When the married couple and their dog moved on, I repeated it to myself: enjoy it. In 14 or 15 years, perhaps even sooner, that little one will break your heart. Your whole life up until that point will revolve around it: its barking, its tail-wagging, its smell, its love of swimming, its dreams, and the way it gradually slows down once both of you are past your prime.

Many dog owners get a sudden fright when they finally realise that their pet is getting old. Strangely, our dog's age tends to dawn on us sooner than our own.

What can we do about it? Should we sit there like rabbits in the headlights, mourning the passing of time and waiting for death? We don't know when it's coming. It could be today, tomorrow or not for seven or eight years. We have no control over it. What we can do, though, is live and love to the full. And make every moment with our pets the most precious moment of our lives. Because that moment is all that matters.

The Bible says, "Where your treasure is, there your heart will be."[14] The order is important here: our hearts follow the things we prize, not the other way round. Unfortunately too many people set their hearts on the wrong things. We don't find proper, lasting fulfilment in transitory things, but in the things that give us real joy and a meaningful purpose: our families, our friends, and our values. Old dogs have more or less identical needs to us. Above all, they want to be loved, and they want to have somebody to love. Their attachment to their human beings is so strong that they value verbal praise from them even more than food.

This was proved in an experiment conducted by Gregory S. Berns of Emory University in Atlanta, Georgia.[15] He led a team of researchers testing how dog brains respond to different rewards. First of all, he trained the animals to lie down in an MRI scanner of their own free will and stay still during the scan – in itself a spectacular achievement on the dogs' part. Anyone who's had an MRI scan knows how noisy the machine is. Next, the 15 canine guinea pigs learned to associate three objects with particular outcomes: a pink toy car meant food, a blue knight meant verbal praise from their owner, and a hairbrush brought no reward. The scientists tested which items activated the dogs' reward centres most strongly.

The results showed that dogs are not by any means just out for treats. Most favoured their owner's praise over food. These same preferences were exhibited once again in a behavioural experiment. The dogs were put in a simple maze, and had to decide between one of two paths: the first led to a bowl full of treats, the second to their owner, who greeted their dog enthusiastically when it arrived.

"We demonstrated how important praise is for a dog – social reward seems to have a similar meaning for them as it does for us humans," Berns concluded.

Dogs have adapted to us like no other animal. They can identify our emotions and even interpret our expressions. Knowing that praise can be more important than food, even for a greedy labrador, should make us humans proud. It seems we've done something right in our relationships.

And we give them the same love in return, in that we give up a lot and are prepared to take on a significant amount for them. That was clear from the many letters I received from owners of old or sick dogs, who wrote to me when I asked readers of my online newsletter to tell me their stories.

Ulrich's old dog Linda has an aversion to snow. Following heavy snowfall, Linda considers it imperative for her owner to go out and heap the snow into a big pile in the garden at once.

But Ulrich lives in Bavaria, where it snows regularly. "Every winter I have to dig up entire streets with a snow shovel – including crossroads and roundabouts – before madam can finally settle down." Anything for the dog.

My friend Annelie is a businesswoman. She let her two old rescue dogs Max and Juma "choose" her new car. The oldies had to be able to get in easily, so Annelie and her husband took the dogs along to various garages, all the way from Porsche to Mercedes, and insisted that the dogs be allowed to test the cars. "The colour drained from the salesman's face when jet-black Max got into a Mercedes E-Class and made himself comfy on the white leather seats," Annelie giggles. On balance, though, it's probably worth it for the salesman if he ends up shifting a Porsche Cayenne.

Anya, the owner of husky crossbreed Olmo, went even further: she bought herself a "dog-friendly" cottage in the country, so that Olmo could enjoy the final years of his life on one floor, with a large garden to boot. Of course, these are extreme examples. But they show how far we are prepared to go to make our dogs happy.

But we don't really need to go to that much effort. Last spring I took Shira on holiday to the seaside. I was exhausted and run down and desperately needed some time out. I booked a cottage in Denmark at short notice. I had decided to focus entirely on my old girl and to do things her way. Holiday à la Shira.

I watched her. She'd make a yogi jealous. When she got tired, she went to sleep – even in the middle of a busy restaurant. When she wanted to play, she snatched up her ball and dropped it into my lap, whatever the weather. When she was thirsty, she had a drink, and when she was hungry, she stood in front of me for an age, giving me this *look* until I got up with a sigh and went to get her some food. After a long beach walk, I spread out a rug in a corner of the terrace and we settled down in the sun. I smelt the sea, listened to the waves, felt the sun on my face and my dog's warm fur in my hands. Life couldn't get any better.

For years the Danes have ranked among the happiest people in the world, according to the *World Happiness Report*.[16] Their magic word is currently in vogue. The word is "hygge", which means something like "cosiness and comfort". For me, those few days were perfect doggy-hygge.

5

You Don't Have to Be Perfect

———————

Their names are Quasimodo, Sweepee Rambo and Icky, and they have one thing in common: they are all what we would, by modern beauty standards, consider "ugly": bristly, furless, toothless, hairless, with oversized ears, lolling tongues and different-coloured eyes. By contrast with all the identical, picture-perfect puppies that we fawn over in magazines, these creatures have unique, expressive and even humanlike features. A whiskered terrier sticking out its tongue is the spitting image of a playful old physicist. A frizzy-haired dog with its eyes shut and a wry smile on its face looks just like a cocky teenager.

Quasimodo and his pals travel to California each year for the "World's Ugliest Dog Contest". The winner gets $1,500. The 2017 champion was Martha, a three-year-old Neapolitan mastiff weighing in at 57kg.[17] Martha decided the prizegiving ceremony was the perfect time to have a snooze, and snored noisily as she was declared the winner, totally unfazed by the audience or the venue. The judges chose her because of her "sweet nature, lumbering gait and dangly jowls". When I look at pictures of other participants on the internet, I honestly don't know whether I'm meant to find them actually ugly or kind of sweet.

The organisers of the competition make a point of emphasising that the prize isn't intended to make fun of the dogs. Rather, it is intended to celebrate the beauty of all animals, regardless of their supposed imperfections. Like most dogs on the 2017 list, Martha came from a rescue home.

Many of these dogs would presumably have had no chance of being adopted if it hadn't been for kind-hearted people who didn't care about outward appearances – people who saw with their hearts instead. Don't we all want to be loved like that?

Dogs couldn't care less about their appearance. They don't compare themselves with other animals. Can you imagine a labrador wishing he had a fox terrier's ears? Or a bulldog wanting to be a greyhound, or a poodle being jealous of a collie's hairdo? We humans sacrifice precious time and a great deal of money altering our appearance in our constant search for self-improvement and perfection. And then we become frustrated and unhappy when our unrealistic beauty standards and personal goals remain out of reach. We long for the perfect body and flawless skin, instead of simply valuing our own unique features.

I love looking at elderly people. Look at the face of a hundred-year-old. Marked and furrowed by the years, it has become a mirror of that person's life, grabbing your attention like a painting. How boring an immaculate face is by comparison!

In her book *Dog Years: Faithful Friends, Then & Now*, Amanda Jones presents the portraits and stories of 30 dogs.[18] There are two photographs of each dog, one as a puppy on the left-hand page and another as an old dog on the right-hand page. It is fascinating that, over all that time, their personalities don't seem to have changed – they have simply become more ingrained with age. Dogs at the beginning of their lives and at the end – and yet their expressions remain the same.

An old dog's face is unmistakable: sties, warts, broken or missing teeth. Sometimes their eyes have dimmed – all evidence of a life lived to the full, but also of the struggles of old age.

At 13, my Shira is no longer the enchanting puppy dog that everyone wanted to stroke in the street – thank God. To me, of course, she's still the loveliest dog in the world, a living work of art, a constant reminder of nature's extraordinary powers, a beauty on four paws. And to herself? She doesn't want to be anything other than what she is: a retriever. It's in her genes. If I throw a ball, she chases after it, brings it back, drops it into my hands, and waits for me to throw it again. Her instincts prevent her biting down hard when she's carrying something in her mouth. We bred retrievers as hunting dogs, training them to fetch ducks out of water without damaging them. Swimming and retrieving are Shira's calling. She's happy as she is, and never tries to be anything else. I didn't have to train her to be herself. For her, swimming is as natural as breathing. I couldn't leave her in the middle of a field of sheep and expect her to herd them. She isn't a sheepdog, and never will be. She's about as likely to pull a sleigh.

Dog owners nowadays make big demands of their pets. They have to look good, heed our every command, and be the most loveable creature around. That's a heavy burden for them – and us – to bear.

Shira is the third dog I've owned. When I got Klops, my first dog, I had no idea how to train him, and did pretty much everything wrong. He lived a free, independent life – the nicest way I can think of to describe a bullish, obstinate dog – and I didn't think my (or his) mistakes were the end of the world. By the time I got Lady, I'd learned my lesson, and tried to train her better. Shira was supposed to be perfect. Personal experience suggested that she had to learn everything in her first year, so that I could approach the next 12 to 14 years with calm. So

I took Shira to a puppy group, then to a young dogs' group, then to a retrieving course. I gave her new names: Shira-No and Shira-Off-The-Sofa. Then she hit puberty and her hard drive was wiped overnight. Nothing worked anymore. But we got through that, too.

In the end she did become my dream dog, but I was so exhausted that I could hardly enjoy her perfection. Only when I decided to relax the reins and accept her imperfections did we start having fun with one another again. The rules changed. Rather than "The dog isn't allowed on the sofa," I decided, "The sofa's okay if her blanket's on it." Meanwhile my dog claimed her own armchair, which she can still climb into even in her old age.

At some point after that first exhausting year, I gave up my training methods. Shira knows the most important commands (Stop! Come here! Sit! Stay!) – the ones that keep her safe in the world. That's all she needs. No living creature should be constantly kept in check by commands and gestures. That's not how wolves train their young. Young wolves are allowed to forge their own experiences and make their own mistakes, even if they have to deal with the possible consequences. I once saw this in action while observing a family of wolves in Yellowstone.[19] For days, a dozy young wolf had been annoying its family, constantly dawdling when the pack was on the move, lingering behind to sniff at something or other that it considered more important than them. Every time, the others had to wait for him to catch up again. But at some point they decided enough was enough. The wolves moved on, leaving the daydreamer behind. When he realised they'd gone without him, he started to panic, letting out long, piercing howls, trying to call them back. That had always worked before, but this time it yielded no results. It wasn't until the evening that the family of wolves came back to collect the visibly relieved runt. He had learned his lesson and stuck with the pack from then on.

That's the wolf method: there are no strict rules, the young ones can do what they want, but they soon learn that their every action has consequences. So I decided to train Shira the wolf way. I didn't want her to be a robot; I wanted a dog with creativity, ingenuity and independence. I wanted her to be my equal.

Now Shira has become mutinous in her old age, and I'm glad of it. She ignores me when I call her (it was selective hearing at first, though now she really is deaf). When she throws herself after a rabbit, I'm impressed. Hooray! She can still run when she wants to – who cares if her supposed prey is laughing at the old girl? At the ripe old age of 12, she nicked a sausage off the kitchen table for the first time ever. How on earth did she manage that?

I'm happy that Shira isn't perfect in every way anymore, because that is what makes her so... well, how should I put it... human. I'm proud that she is well trained and that I can take her anywhere. But I love her most of all because she has a mind of her own.

After all, do dogs really have to be perfect? The demands we make of our pets (and of ourselves) vary, and depend on the situation we find ourselves in. There are times when we have to keep our pets under control. And there are other times when we can slacken the reins and turn a blind eye. There are more important things than perfection.

To complicate matters, I am unfortunately a huge perfectionist, and can sometimes be my own worst enemy. As an author, I am always fighting against myself. My manuscripts are never good enough: I'm always convinced that I could have done a better job. If the book subsequently does well, I can hardly enjoy it. Instead of being happy with my achievements, I scrutinise the bestseller list or the Amazon rankings and start working myself up if I'm "falling". With each new book I put myself under fresh pressure – it has to be at least as good as the previous one. It's all too easy for me to stop myself enjoying my own success. I whinge about my first-world problems, telling myself that I used to be freer and more creative when I could just write how I wanted, without so much pressure – and I fail to recognise that I am becoming a slave to my own search for perfection, a perfection that I will never achieve. I measure my success against other people, forcing myself into a perpetual struggle against an opponent I can never defeat.

In her book *The Artist's Way*, the author Julia Cameron wrote, "Perfectionism is a refusal to let yourself move ahead."[20]

There will never be a "perfect" book. At some point I have to accept that I have written the best book I possibly can. Then I must stop writing and get on with my next project. Letting go is an important part of creativity.

As of late, more and more people have been aiming for absolute self-perfection. They want to sleep less, work more productively, live better lives, be happier and healthier, maintain a strong relationship, and use their time more effectively. To stay true to this goal, people monitor themselves round the clock with technology, wearing sensors on their bodies and downloading programmes onto their laptops and apps onto their phones that will help them achieve optimal results. Even at night, some people wear headbands to monitor their brain activity, so that in the morning their smartphone can tell them if they got a good and restful (that is, productive) night's sleep.

But recently a new trend has been developing, even among fanatical self-improvers: the "cheat day".[21] On a cheat day you're allowed to have a proper feast, before exercising restraint again over the following six days. Especially suitable for dieters, it is designed to release tension and reward you for the discipline you've shown throughout the week. It is interesting to note that people who include a cheat day as part of their diet still lose weight and change their eating habits in the long term.

This crossed my mind when I was sitting in an ice cream shop with Shira recently. Three women were having a chat at the table next to us. One of them was gazing gloomily into a cup of green tea on the table in front of her, telling the others about her new diet. "No sugar, no fat, no carbs. I've already lost 10 kilos," she announced triumphantly. But unlike me, her friends didn't seem particularly impressed.

"And what's the point of that?" one of them asked. "You don't look very happy." She scooped up a mountain of vanilla ice cream and whipped cream onto her spoon, picked out a glacé cherry with her fingers, and balanced it artistically on top.

"Just imagine, you spend months going without all those delicious things to become slim and beautiful, and then you go out of your front door one day and get hit by a lorry." She moved the spoon slowly from side to side, right under her friend's nose, before turning it around and shoving it into her own mouth. "Mmm." She licked her lips. "You should definitely have gone for the ice cream."

The three women looked at each other for a moment and then exploded with laughter. As they ordered a third sundae, I slipped Shira a scoop of vanilla to lick. I like to indulge her whenever we go to the ice cream shop.

Dogs don't care about being the slimmest, the best, or the most beautiful creatures in the world. They're content with the gifts nature gave them. This makes their lives simple and straightforward. Nobody's perfect. We all have the odd blemish here or there. What does it matter? Isn't that exactly what makes us individuals? The fact that we're all different?

Shira sometimes limps. She's been doing it for as long as I can remember. To this day I still don't know why. It happens occasionally when we're out and about.

Two women with Nordic walking sticks stop and look at her sympathetically. "Oh look, poor creature. Is he hurt?"

"No, *she* isn't. She's just a bit bonkers," I reply, ignoring Shira's disapproving glare.

When they're gone, I say to her, "I'm right. You *are* bonkers."

"No I'm not!"

"Yes you are!"

"No I'm not!"

"You are. Just now you tried to scratch your left shoulder with your left hind leg while walking along. You know you can't manage on three legs."

"Pfff…"

"Got an itch?" I scratch her shoulder, and she leans enthusiastically into my hand.

"Nah!"

"Do you know how much I've spent on all kinds of vets, just to find out if there's anything actually wrong with you? None of them could explain why you scratch yourself like that. But you still do it. So you must be bonkers. Officially."

If Shira was a person, she'd shrug her shoulders at this point and carry on walking. "Well, that's that then. Let's see how you cope."

"But you know what? I love you even though you're bonkers – maybe even because of it."

A vital part of our search for perfection is our desire to be loved. We think our quirks and errors of judgment make us inadequate. Dogs know better. They are simply themselves. Perhaps that's why they're so ready to show affection. To them, we're perfect as we are – flawed, weak, highly eccentric, but always deserving of love.

It's important to recognise that what gives our lives meaning is not our accomplishments, our appearance, or our achievements, but the depth and truth of our relationships with the people and creatures around us.

A terrifying proportion of my life has passed me by while I've been busy struggling for perfection. But now I know that "perfect" means safe, restrained, and rule-bound – and to me that all sounds boring. I'm more attracted to chaos and glorious imperfection. Accepting your own shortcomings means being true to yourself instead of worrying about appearances. It means giving credence to the (downright revolutionary) idea that the world is beautiful and precious just as it is, and that you don't need to change it or spice it up to make it better.

So Shira and I blunder through the world as we find it. We sit on the sand, dance in the rain and listen to the rustling of dry leaves as the wind blows them over the pavement. Here and now. Who needs perfection when they can live truthfully, with open eyes and an open heart?

6

Regret Nothing

....

Every morning I read the local paper over breakfast, and usually end up flicking through the death announcements on the last page. Has anyone I know died? Is it my age group's turn yet? Or have I got away with it again?

This morning I discover an announcement with the heading "… And we thought we had so much time left". I swallow and cast a swift glance at Shira, who is snoozing in her basket. How sad that some people never manage to fulfil their potential – if they spend their lives making plans for "later" and "later" never comes. I don't know how old the person was when they died. I can't see a date of birth, but the heading wouldn't make sense for an old person, so they must have been relatively young. For the loved ones they left behind, their regrets about what could have been evidently outweigh their joy and gratitude for the time they got to spend together.

The Australian author Bronnie Ware wrote a bestseller entitled *The Top Five Regrets of the Dying*.[22] She spent time with dying people as they looked back on their lives and told her what they regretted and what they wished they'd done better or differently. The five most important lessons were:

1. Live a life true to yourself, not the life other people expect of you.
2. Don't work so hard.
3. Express your feelings.
4. Stay in touch with your friends.
5. Let yourself be happy.

In the book the author tells the story of Grace, who never managed to take her life into her own hands and be true to herself. When she was dying, she could hardly bear to think how she'd let her husband terrorise her all her life, just because she wanted to project an image of a well-functioning marriage. Who for? By the time she asked herself this question, it was too late.

Gerhard, a friend of mine, lost his wife to cancer. He was inconsolable because he'd always told her he had work to do whenever she wanted to talk. And he bitterly regretted that he could never open up to her, though he'd known that was what she longed for more than anything.

Do old dogs ever ask themselves why they did one thing or failed to do another? No, presumably not. They live in the present. Every dog owner knows that's why it is so pointless to punish Fido when you come home from work to find he's dissected your new slippers into bite-size chunks. He simply wouldn't make the connection between the punishment and his forbidden love of chewing. Dogs can't have any regrets. They are the embodiment of self-acceptance. We humans beat ourselves up far too often with what-ifs and if-onlys, especially when we realise our time is running out.

When I got Lady, I had grand plans for us: long walks and month-long breaks together. But something always got in the way. John Lennon was right: "Life is what happens to you while you're busy making other plans."

With Shira I wanted that to change, and when she was a puppy I had all the time in the world for her. Then she got older, and each December I promised her that we would do amazing things in the new year. No more Alpine mountain crossings, perhaps, but there were plenty more exciting trips to be made.

And still life passed me by. My wolf research in Yellowstone took me away to America for weeks at a time, though Shira enjoyed her time with my parents while I was away. Lectures, seminars, I was on the move a lot – and I missed my dog terribly. Cuddles with other dogs are a comfort, but they're not the same. And now? Now Shira is far too old for hour-long walks. I wish with all my might that I could turn back the clock just a little.

But it is what it is. I can only change the present. And that's what I did when I realised how much of my time with Shira I'd already missed.

I had already quit my job as a lawyer to study wolves. Not only because I was extremely frustrated at work, but because I didn't want to reach the end of my life and ask myself, "Why didn't you follow your dreams?"

The meaning of life is having no regrets. If I fell down dead today, I'd go out with a smile on my face, because I've lived my life to the full. I have passed through deep valleys and conquered high peaks. All of that has brought me to where I am now. Of course I regret some things in my life, especially the times when I have walked out on people or hurt somebody close to me. There's nothing I would rather do than ask their forgiveness. But I can't ask them all, because some aren't around anymore. And the older I get, the fewer opportunities I have to put things right.

I would like to talk to the people who have hurt me and ask them why they did it. But usually I lack the courage, or they've already died or moved away, or perhaps they simply don't want to talk. So in the end all I can do is forgive them in my heart.

My desire to follow my dreams and have no regrets then led me to embark on the greatest adventure of my life – when I fell head over heels in love with a stranger and moved to Minnesota to live in the wild with him.[23] I met Greg at a seminar on wolves, and was fascinated by his life in the middle of wolf and bear country, with no electricity or running water. This man was living *my* dream. That was how I'd always imagined I'd spend my life. So I went to live with him.

I stayed with my wild man for most of a year – interrupted only by short trips home, so as not to jeopardise my visitor visa. It was an unimaginably tough and deprived way of life, but it was a life of such beauty that it still takes my breath away thinking about it today. The -30°C nights, lying in my sleeping bag underneath the dancing northern lights, with the song of the wolves all around us – that made up for all the negatives, as did my numerous close encounters with wild wolves.

Ultimately it was the daily routine that was my undoing. Refusals to compromise, increasing friction, and a whirlwind of resentment between us forced me to flee the wild.

The worst thing for me, though, was that when I moved to be with Greg, I couldn't take my dog Lady with me. I could manage a few weeks in America without her, but I hadn't been expecting to stay for ever. Greg disliked dogs, though, and I bowed to his will.

Minnesota and the natural world that became my home fascinated and bewitched me. Today I know that I was less in love with Greg than I was with the life he led. He symbolised a dream that I wanted to follow. I wanted to move to the wild for the same reasons as the writer and naturalist Henry David Thoreau – "to live deliberately, to front only the essential facts of life, and see if I could learn what it had to teach."[24] I wanted to find out who I was, what drove me, where my boundaries were and how capable I was of appreciating nature. Like Thoreau, I wanted "to anticipate not the sunrise and the dawn merely, but nature herself." Through Greg, I could make this dream come true, though eventually I realised a life like that wasn't what I really wanted.

I now know that the reality of living in a log cabin is nowhere near as romantic as I'd imagined. But surviving in the wild does teach us how little we actually need to get by. If our existence is reduced to the bare essentials, other things become important to us and we begin to discover our real selves.

Living with Greg stirred something within me that had always been there, but that I had never grasped until then. I had always longed to live in a cabin in the wilderness. Thanks to him, I got to live my dream.

My year in Minnesota shaped the rest of my life: I later went back into the wild to live with wolves, alone this time.

Eventually I had to say goodbye to my dream. But I said it with a grateful smile, because the only thing worse than letting go of a dream is never realising it in the first place.

Do I regret my time in the wild? Not one bit. What I do regret, though, is not fighting my dog's corner and insisting on taking her with me. Perhaps she wouldn't have survived long out there, in close proximity with large predators. But I still feel I betrayed her. Do I wish I'd done things differently? Of course. But what's the point? I did the best I could at the time, in the circumstances and with the resources I had. I can't know what my life would have been like if I'd acted differently. The fact is: this is where I am now. Everything I've seen and done, or not done, has made me the person I am today. So every "what if" is meaningless.

And what about my life with Shira? Have I lived *our* life together to the full? Or have I missed a large part of it and wasted precious time?

I look at her and ask her, "Is there anything you regret? Is there anything I should have done differently?"

My golden girl gives me a cheerful grin. "No regrets!"

She's right. The present is all we have. While I've been writing this chapter, Shira has been making her presence felt. She wakes up, scratches herself, stands up, shakes herself, walks once around my desk, and then comes over and nudges me.

"In a minute. Just need to finish this chapter," I'm about to say. Then I catch myself in the act. I get up, settle down on the floor with her and throw the ball she's brought me. I know that one day I'll long to have moments like these back. To interrupt my work for a cuddle with my dog. Yes, death is standing just behind me and looking over my shoulder. But today death has a smile on his face. And I smile back, because I know he is a font of wisdom in matters of life and love.

We all live with feelings of guilt in one form or another. Thoughts like "if only I had…" or "I wish I could…" torment us, especially if we live with an animal whose lifespan is so short and who offers us nothing but unconditional love. We tell ourselves we have failed as human beings, as partners, and we don't have much time left to rectify our mistakes.

When we hold our dying dog in our arms one day, we will regret every walk we didn't go on, every stroke we didn't give, every cuddle we turned down, every telling-off, every time we said "later". And we will wish we could do it all again. But it's no use beating ourselves up. Apart from anything else, the dog won't be thinking like that at all – they will long since have forgiven us.

"Okay, you didn't want to go for a walk yesterday? Doesn't matter. Let's go NOW. A bit of rain won't do any harm." That's what Shira would say. Or, "No cuddles yesterday, so what? No harm done. Come to the sofa."

Regret Nothing

We can't live our lives if we constantly regret the past or if we are frightened of the future. Old dogs teach us that the important thing isn't what we've *not* done, but what we have done or what we're doing today. Today we can have fun, show love, do something nice for an animal or a person, and make the world a better place.

Forgive as Long as You Live

In a park somewhere in a city, a group of dogs are playing energetically. They run around, jump up, and chase after one another. Then someone throws a ball into the crowd, and they all go for it at once. Within seconds, the happy pack transforms into a raging mob. The dogs become a blur of bodies, snarling, barking and yelping. It's dreadful to watch. Just as their concerned owners rush in to intervene, one of the dogs skips out of the war zone, proudly carrying the trophy in his mouth. The rest of them dash after him and chase him around the park. The expression of the victorious dog morphs from one of grim determination into a triumphant grin. It's just a game, and he's having fun. Within a very short space of time, the mood is good again.

For dogs, forgiveness and "making up" takes a matter of minutes. When two of them get into a quarrel, the matter will soon be settled, with no bitterness or hurt feelings. Dogs aren't vindictive – in fact, humans are probably the only living beings who bear grudges. Here's one way to put this to the test: lock your spouse and your dog out of the house in the pouring rain for half an hour. Then let them both back in. Which of them greets you more enthusiastically?

Forgiveness is one of the most unnatural challenges we have to face in the world. Let's be honest – if someone hurts us, we want justice, fairness and retribution above all else. A friend of mine was left by her husband when he fell for someone else. She took it so badly that she became physically ill. As a result, she lost her job and had to rebuild her life from scratch. The most painful thing about it for her was that her husband's new partner was (in her opinion) not nearly as attractive as her. And throughout her marriage she had made it her absolute priority to look good, in order to hold on to her younger husband and keep him committed to her. But then he fell in love with a rival who wasn't as slim or as beautiful. That wounded my friend's pride more than anything else. How could he do that? What did he see in her?

When I asked her husband about his new partner, he confided in me: "She makes me laugh. She's relaxed, and I feel secure around her."

After the separation, my friend's life as she knew it fell apart. Instead of looking to the future, she let herself lapse into hatred and bitterness. In response to my question whether she could forgive her husband and let it go, she gave an indignant no. She would never forgive him.

Forgiveness is something we consider often enough, but actually going through with it can be very difficult. If we make things easy for ourselves by not forgiving other people, we can carry on blaming them for how we feel. We can let ourselves remain victims, like my friend. The hurt she suffered resulted from her disappointed expectations of what her husband should be like. But life and love are simply impossible to predict. Things happen. People are betrayed and promises are broken. The question is: how do we deal with it?

Anger and hatred are an emotional burden. They prevent us moving forward with our lives. Ultimately we only harm ourselves if we are incapable of forgiveness. Forgiveness puts the power back into our own hands. When we forgive, we can find peace and move on. It doesn't mean that we accept how someone has behaved, or that what happened is water under the bridge. But it would be foolish to refuse to forgive. We have all made countless mistakes in our own lives, and have been forgiven. Hopefully.

Britta, another friend of mine, was trapped in an unhappy, controlling relationship. She was scared of leaving her boyfriend. He lied to her and betrayed her, but she was even more scared of being alone than she was of her unhealthy relationship, and she couldn't muster the strength to break up with him. Her only comfort and support was her dog Charly. Sometimes her boyfriend took the dog for a walk when she was at work.

"Charly never wanted to go with him – he seemed afraid of him," she said. "I couldn't understand it, because my boyfriend was always very nice to him when I was around."

When she came home from work one day, her dog was lying whimpering in the corner with a swollen eye. After lengthy questioning, Britta's boyfriend finally admitted that he'd hit Charly because he disobeyed him.

"My world fell apart," she said. "I threw him out straight away."

The worst thing was that a short time later she took him back, because he solemnly promised to mend his ways. And like many women in abusive relationships, Britta wanted to believe him. She forgave him, but never left him alone with her dog again. "I was scared every time I had to go to work, and tried to leave Charly with friends instead. It was awful. My fear of losing my boyfriend was stronger than my love of my dog. I had the constant feeling that I was betraying Charly."

One evening she saw her boyfriend reach out to stroke Charly. "The dog shrank back and looked at me with an expression I will never forget." That was the moment Britta finally decided in favour of her dog. The following morning she packed her bags, and she and Charly moved out. Talking about it now, she is overwhelmed by the memory of it all. Fighting back tears, she tells me, "I failed my dog. He trusted me and I failed him." It was nearly a year until she got over her boyfriend.

Soon enough, Charly was his old self again. But Britta has never forgiven herself. Years later, she still blames herself. To this day – though Charly died years ago – she can't forgive herself for delaying so long. "I have to live with the guilt."

We are human beings, and we make mistakes in our inter-actions with other people and with our dogs. Some of them are so bad that we keep feeling guilty for the rest of our lives. We bury this guilt deep in our hearts, because we're ashamed. We hope that one day it will disappear just like that. But no matter how deep we bury it, unresolved guilt never dies. It lives on. And everything that we bury alive will come to the surface again one day. We must learn to live with guilt, and to forgive ourselves too. Dogs manage it without a second thought. They're the absolute masters of it.

In our lives, things will happen again and again that we simply can't put right, no matter how much we want to. People and animals that we hurt aren't always there anymore. We've missed our chance to ask them for forgiveness. So the important thing is to make sure that we don't treat anyone badly in the here and now. And if we do hurt someone by accident, the most important thing of all is to forgive ourselves.

Could I forgive someone who failed me and betrayed me? I don't know. But I am sure that Charly long since forgave his owner. Trust was the foundation of their relationship, a trust so strong that forgiveness went without saying. Perhaps we should learn from our canine friends and their big hearts. Nothing we do can make them leave us. They are incapable of condemnation. We can hit them, starve them, and fail to return their affections. But when we call them, they still run to us and welcome our attentions with open hearts.

Our lives in the present shouldn't be defined by our past. Sometimes forgiveness comes easily, sometimes it is unbearably difficult, but it is always, always important: it is the only way we can heal and find freedom again. We all get to a point at some stage in our lives when we must heal old wounds – the ones we have created, as well as the ones others have inflicted on us. Forgiveness doesn't mean "Forget it" or "It doesn't matter". It is a process that takes time and effort. You can't force it. If someone has hurt me, eventually I choose not to hold it against them anymore. I forgive them so that we can both get on with our lives. And that's largely for my own sake. Having constant grounds to complain doesn't get you anywhere. You have to let go and move on.

Our dogs are a shining example of how to ask someone's forgiveness.

My mongrel Klops' eyesight started to go in his old age. One day, he playfully snapped at a stick that I was holding in my hand, but missed, and accidentally bit my hand. He was inconsolable, hopping around me with his tail between his legs, licking my hand and my face.

"Oh my God, what on earth have I done? I'm so sorry. I'm so, so sorry."

I had to reassure him. "It wasn't your fault. It's okay." Only then did he calm down.

We should forgive our dogs as easily as they forgive us. Love is all that counts. Dogs can let bygones be bygones and embrace every new day.

And let's not forget there are sometimes legitimate reasons why dogs (and humans) bite. Sometimes it's in self-defence. We can't always know why they did what they did. If we respect that and respond sympathetically, if we can give them the benefit of the doubt, then we open the door to understanding, and can ultimately find peace.

Shira is snoring. I sit in silence, listening to her, feeling my best friend breathing in and out. I close my eyes and let my fingers glide through her fur. A moment suspended in time. The longer we live with a dog, the more "if-only" feelings we have. When I'm with Shira, I have twinges of conscience about every day, every minute that I didn't spend with her. But I know I've done the best I can. And that is what I will continue to do. That is good enough.

You Are
Important

Following the publication of my book *The Wisdom of Wolves*,
I was invited onto a talk show with the famous German
TV host Markus Lanz. I was very excited. I'm a regular
viewer, and know that Lanz likes to dig deep – he's very good
at rattling politicians. Would an author like me pass the test?

But my worries were totally unfounded. When we spoke
beforehand, I felt completely at ease, and I forgot all my fears
ahead of the show itself. Lanz has a gift that's rare among
humans, but a lot more common among dogs: he's a great
listener. I hope Mr Lanz doesn't mind me comparing him to
my dog, but that is honestly the greatest compliment I could

give a person. In conversation, Lanz concentrates entirely on his interviewee, and is fully present throughout. Go and watch some old recordings of his show on YouTube, and pay attention to his body language. He looks everyone in the eye, nods his head encouragingly, and… listens. I'm not a psychologist or a body language expert – I can only relay how I felt as a guest.

There are few people in the world who are so attentive to the people they meet. People used to say the same of former US President Bill Clinton: those who spoke to him often remarked how receptive he seemed.

How often do our thoughts wander when we're talking to other people? *So much to do. Everything's going wrong. What did you say?* But that isn't true of dogs – particularly old dogs. While puppies and young dogs are constantly jumping up, eager to explore all the exciting possibilities life has to offer, old dogs focus their full attention on the person they're with. They've already seen it all.

When I'm with Shira, when I talk to her, she listens to me – at least it looks like it. She's deaf, of course. She holds my gaze, her ears prick up, she cocks her head slightly. I have her full attention: I'm important! Shira – like many dogs – has the gift of making her companion feel valued. We can learn to do the same.

A British study in the journal *Scientific Reports* confirms that dogs intensify their facial expressions when they have our attention.[25] The biologist Juliane Kaminski and her team from Portsmouth University conducted experiments with 24 family dogs of different breeds. The dogs used more facial expressions, particularly the dog version of raised eyebrows, when humans were looking at them. The researchers proposed that imitative expressions of this sort could be targeted attempts at communication on the dogs' part.

The scientists carried out an experiment in which they put the dogs in four different situations: first, a human turns to the dog with or without a treat in their hand; next, they turn their back to the dog with or without a treat. In each of these four scenarios, the dogs' facial expressions were filmed.

The result: the dogs altered their facial expression far more when the humans turned towards them. Surprisingly, the presence or absence of a treat didn't make any difference at all, according to the researchers. "We have demonstrated that dogs' production of facial expressions is subject to audience effects... and are not simple emotional displays based on the dogs' arousal state," Kaminski said. The study suggests that facial expressions are an active attempt at communication, and not just an emotional reflex.

So, dogs do what good partners do: they are highly attentive and interested in their humans.

I couldn't take Shira with me on my last work trip: the long train journeys would be too much for her. So I took her to my mother's. As I closed the door behind me, she looked after me sadly. Five minutes later I realised that I'd forgotten something, and went back again. Shira greeted me as if I'd come back from a round-the-world trip. What's going on in her head at moments like that? Does she think I've performed a miracle of some kind? Her joy is overwhelming. It doesn't matter how long I've been gone for – five minutes or two weeks. She greets me in the same way every time: the moment I come through the door, Shira jumps up and grabs the nearest toy. She can never say hello to anyone without bringing them a ball or a toy – that would be a strict breach of labrador protocol. She dashes towards me with the toy in her mouth, and swivels around in circles. Her tail spins like a propeller. Her body pulses with excitement. Wouldn't anyone be touched by a greeting like that? A dog skyrockets your self-confidence into the clouds every time they see you. You can say any old nonsense to your dog and it will look at you and reply, "Hmm, yes, you're right. I'd never thought about it like that before."

We all long to be loved and accepted for who we are. Of all living creatures, dogs are the best at making us feel that way. Dogs don't care about our appearance, income or social status. All they want is to be close to us. This unique form of affection is immensely restorative. We all need it.

As our time together continues to run out, I want more and more to show Shira how important she is to me. If I need to go anywhere without her, I kneel down beside her and tell her where I'm off to. I hug and kiss her before leaving the room.

"Back soon." At home I often interrupt my work to stroke her. I don't want to miss any opportunity to show my affection for her. That would make some hardcore dog trainers' skin crawl. But I don't do it just for Shira – I do it for my own sake too.

That said, it would be sad to think that we only choose to get close to our dogs when we realise our time is running out. Shouldn't we try to live like that all the time? And not just around dogs, but in our relationships with other people too? Shouldn't we keep telling the people in our lives again and again how much we love them? Shouldn't we hug our friends just for the sake of it? Displays of affection can have a powerful impact in any relationship. The problem is that most of us are too busy with our own lives for it to cross our minds. But Shira teaches me the overwhelming power of gratitude.

What would it be like if, just for once, you behaved like a dog when your partner came home?

- You drop whatever you're doing and greet them with a hug.
- You take a real interest in them.
- If they want to talk, you're there for them and give them your full attention.
- You listen to their frustrations without immediately suggesting your own "solutions".
- If they can't meet your needs, you don't get angry with them and don't give up on them.

Is that too much to ask of ourselves? That is exactly what dogs give us every day. They assuage our fears and reduce our stress. And we're not even the same species!

Just being there for one another isn't always enough. In our daily lives there are plenty of people who only remember us for our failings and mistakes, and all too often, we only see the negatives in other people. Why can't we just try seeing them through the eyes of a dog? Look for the good in them? Nobody is born bad. We are all products of our times and our experiences. We could start with our own family and recognise the things that we love about them.

Shira is a great teacher in this regard. Whenever she looks at me, she identifies me as *the* most important person in her life. Her enthusiasm never fails to warm my heart. And for my part, I try my hardest to be nice to the people I meet. It's really not that difficult. A bit of friendliness, openness and thoughtfulness towards our fellow human beings. A thankyou, a smile – that's all.

Love
Unconditionally

A dog to its human:

I can't speak, but I know how to listen.

It's not difficult to make me happy: a walk in the woods and I'll be on top of the world.

I wouldn't mind a treat or two, but I don't want to ask too much.

You don't have to pretend around me. As if I'll ever pretend around you.

When I'm happy, sad or nervous, or bored or ashamed, or if I'm feeling sorry for myself, you'll see it in my face.

I won't make a secret of myself. You'll know it's me when I start barking loudly the moment you come through the door. I just can't contain myself.

I can smell fear and love from a mile off.
I always know how you're feeling, and I'm quite good at adapting to it.
I'll lick your face when you're sad.
I'll cuddle you when you deserve it.
I'll give you a paw when you need it.
And if anything else is up, you'll see it in my eyes.
I'll always be at your side, and you'll never be alone.

That is a dog's love.

"Unbelievable, isn't it? They love you no matter what!" says a convicted gangster in the film *Underdogs*, in which prisoners train guide dogs as part of a rehabilitation initiative.[26]

Dogs are a symbol of unconditional love. They are always happy to see us, even if we're cross with them for something they've done. They forgive us no matter how badly we treat them. It's incredibly difficult to love others without holding back at all. But our furry friends show us how it's done.

As dog owners, we often feel like members of some secret organisation that nobody else understands. This feeling is even stronger if there are old dogs in our lives. Young dogs and puppies are a delight, and you don't have to be a "dog person" to be enchanted by them. But as owners of older, less "attractive" dogs – animals finally showing signs of age – we sometimes feel we have to justify the strength of our bond, or at least rationalise it, though we don't really know how.

How could I possibly explain Shira's place in my heart? Plenty of people find such an intense relationship with an animal peculiar, or at least a bit eccentric.

Try telling someone how happy you are with your dog and how vibrant your relationship feels. They'll probably suggest you see a therapist. You're projecting human love onto an animal – how perverse. You're humanising an animal or using your dog to get over your lonely childhood – how pitiful and sad of you.

When children love dogs it's cute and acceptable, because having a dog teaches them about responsibility. And old people are allowed to be fond of their furry companions as a form of medication or therapy. But the rest of us can kindly get a grip and stop making such a spectacle – it's just a dog!

If we live with young dogs, our relationships revolve around keeping up with them and training them. As they get older, the time we spend with them becomes more important. We take care of our pets, adjusting to their pace and their needs.

I recently met up with some friends in town. We went to a pizzeria and decided to sit outside. Suddenly I felt Shira looking at me. Without a word, I got up, fetched her blanket from the boot of the car, and spread it out on the floor. As she settled down, I looked up to see my friends staring at me in astonishment. "Too hard on her old bones…" I mumbled, shrugging my shoulders. Why did I feel I needed to excuse such a simple act of care?

Love is what matters – simple, unconditional, mutual love. A bond on that level is practically unheard of among humans, because it is fundamentally unspoken. It is not always smooth and straightforward; love can be complicated. But nor is it any less valuable just because one party happens to be furry and walks (or limps) on all fours.

Love is love, human or animal. Being around our dogs makes us feel good. When I come home from the shops, there's a creature waiting to greet me as if the sun has just come up. Shira's whole body is like one big smile. Her tail beats on the floor, her eyes sparkle and assume a clear, profound expression that says, "You're home! Amazing! I'm so happy!"

The world is a better place for it. I scratch her tummy and tell her how much I've missed her, and she puts her forepaws on my forearm. She looks at me, and I return her gaze. In those moments my heart fills up – a blissful, forceful feeling that still moves me after 13 years.

Dogs satisfy our need for closeness and love more or less unconditionally. A real bond like that is a pipe dream for many people these days. Dogs offer us a relationship in which we call the shots almost exclusively. There is no other creature we can share our lives with so closely without being let down or abandoned.

Before you get a dog, you can hardly imagine what life will be like with it. After you get a dog, you can't imagine life without it. You finally feel understood, accepted and loved! Life without Shira? It is unthinkable how quiet and empty my house would be. How many fewer laughs and smiles there would be, and how much less grounded I would feel without her around. The older she gets, and the longer we live together, the more we grow together – if that's still possible.

Old age changes our dogs and us – physically and emotionally too. They never cease to astonish us with what they are capable of, in terms of loyalty, resilience, trust, and unconditional love.

Sylvia wrote me a message about her 10-year-old golden retriever Sam: "He was always very independent, wanted peace and quiet all the time, and didn't much like being stroked. Now he never lets me out of his sight, and craves closeness and affection. It's as if he wants to make up for what he lost out on in his younger years."

The profound love we feel for our dogs has a cellular quality, as if the central part of you – your whole nervous system – is bound up with the life you have created together. Having a dog reprograms you: you're no longer Mr Miller or Mrs Smith. You're "Rocky's owner" or "the man with the old setter" or "the woman with the blind dalmatian". We dog owners identify ourselves and others by our animals.

Unconditional love. When we hear this phrase, certain images spring to mind: a mother and child, a dog and its owner. A while back, I sent a survey to friends and acquaintances, asking, "Who, in your opinion, is capable of unconditional love?" The overwhelming majority replied, "Dogs".

Dogs absolutely guarantee us their unswerving, limitless loyalty at all times. They don't care what's in it for them. If a dog offers you its friendship, it's yours for life. Dogs don't mind that humans are as faithful as fleas in the mating season, that they are more loyal to their hair products than they are to themselves, and that half of their marriages end in divorce. They will never walk out on their humans. Former American President Harry S. Truman once said, "If you want a friend in Washington, get a dog."[27]

And humans? Are there any circumstances in which we're capable of unconditional love? To a dog, it doesn't matter if you're rich or poor, young or old, whether you're a millionaire with a doctorate or a homeless person on the street. Their whole body will still tremble with excitement when they see you. Do you know anyone else like that?

Let's not kid ourselves. A dog's unconditional love is an ideal – a perfect model of what we think real love should look like. For some people, a pet is the one thing they are not afraid of and that makes them feel valued, which is sad, because we should be able to strike up equally profound relationships with other people. But human relationships are often complicated. We love someone, but we are afraid to show it, fearing that our love will not be returned, or even that we'll be taken advantage of. And so we bottle up our feelings. In these circumstances, it is perhaps easier to look outside our own species to find the perfect relationship – or at least, a relationship that seems perfect to us.

Dogs love us unconditionally and forgive us every single time. The only question they ask is, "Do you love me?" We take dogs' love for granted. If a dog stopped loving a human one day, that person would probably have to spend a lot of time in therapy trying to find out why the dog shut them out.

Arthur Schopenhauer famously said, "As long as I've known human beings, I've loved animals."[28] At first glance, that makes sense to every dog owner, though it makes me feel a little uneasy. How can I love all animals, but hate or vilify other people? Personally, I believe that our animals' love ultimately teaches us to love other human beings with the same goodwill and the same forgiving generosity that our dogs show us every day.

The German poet Rainer Maria Rilke hit the nail on the head: "For one human being to love another: that is perhaps the most difficult of all our tasks... the work for which all other work is just preparation."[29]

Our greatest challenge in life is to learn to love one another as dogs love us. How could we even begin to measure the love dogs give us? If we think about our lives before and after we got a dog, we realise that they have shown us a new world, where we have experienced the true meaning of unconditional love.

As a child, I grew up with my grandparents. Dogs were part and parcel of my family. They lived a simple life, eating cheap food out of cans or getting our leftovers after dinner. We had a kennel in the garden where they spent most of the day. At night they slept on a blanket in my grandparents' bedroom (or occasionally in my bed). They came and went through the house when they felt like it: a completely normal day-to-day existence. They were loved and treasured, but my grandparents didn't make a big fuss of them. Dogs were simply part of the furniture.

My grandfather had a very close relationship with his alsatian Axel, who was also my best friend. He had him properly trained to be a guard dog. That was what dogs were for in those days. The two of them were a great team, and there was never a more gentle, loving dog than Axel. That made my first childhood encounter with death all the more traumatic: Axel was poisoned. No child should ever have to go through anything like that.

For Shira, the world is a friend she is still yet to meet. Like most of her fellow retrievers, she is hyper-sociable. But why is that?

Bridgett vonHoldt and her colleagues from Princeton University found out why.[30] She compared the behaviour of domestic dogs with that of wolves who were accustomed to being around humans. Wolves demonstrated their tenacity and strong problem-solving skills, while dogs turned to humans for help after only a few attempts – even to a stranger if necessary. According to the research, dogs' social streak is a result of a genetic mutation in the sixth chromosome, a mutation that is not present in wolves. In humans, it leads to a genetic disorder known as Williams syndrome, which causes a childlike level of dependency in adults.

Over the course of evolution, human beings began to selectively breed the dogs with this chromosome mutation, won over by their friendliness and mild disposition. A sort of "survival of the friendliest".

But love between humans and dogs derives not only from a genetic process, but also from a simple chemical one. When I look into Shira's eyes, the same thing happens as when a mother and child or a couple look at each other: the levels of the love hormone oxytocin rise in my bloodstream, and the levels of the stress hormone cortisol reduce. We know from experiments with eye trackers that dogs seek eye contact with us above all else.[31] That is how they read our emotions and moods. Old dogs in particular seek regular eye contact with their humans. They hold our gaze, looking deep into our soul. What's more, they are constantly watching us, and adjusting their behaviour accordingly.

Yes, dogs can also be replacement children. Half of all dog owners give them human names. I kiss Shira probably 40 times a day, and touch her more times than I can count. I can't say that of anyone else in my life. I also talk to her a lot. Sometimes I even find myself waiting for an answer. Then I look at her. "You don't have a clue what I'm on about, do you?"

Shira looks at me, alert, curious, and completely clueless. "Of course not. Not the foggiest."

Schopenhauer is right, of course. Anyone who makes a serious attempt to research human behaviour learns to value dogs' company sooner or later. The founder of psycho-analysis, Sigmund Freud, was no exception. At the outset of the Second World War, he was feeling particularly despondent about his fellow human beings. He had spent his whole life analysing the contradictory and irrational aspects of the human subconscious, but by that point it seemed far easier to understand the psyche of animals.

At 72, the expert on the human mind was a latecomer to the mind of the dog. A close friend and benefactor, Princess Marie Bonaparte, transformed the supposed animal-hater into a true dog-lover. His daughter Anna recounts that Freud valued his dogs' grace, humility and loyalty above all else. He believed their greatest advantage over humans was their complete lack of ambivalence. "Dogs," he said, "love their friends and bite their enemies, in stark contrast with humans, who are incapable of pure love and have to intermingle love and hate in all their relationships."

In a letter to Marie Bonaparte shortly before his death, Freud described what dogs had to offer the human race: "a dog offers its master affection without ambivalence, it frees our lives from the unbearable conflicts of civilisation, and it shows us the beauty of existence in itself."[32] I think every dog owner – and above all anyone who has or used to have an old dog – would absolutely agree with the expert.

I am convinced that dogs keep millions of people mentally healthy, when they would otherwise be deeply neurotic in our lonely world. Our dogs connect us with our inner lives. When we look into their eyes, we recognise this connection.

THE DARK SIDE OF LOVE

We give our four-legged friends food, shelter, medical provisions and – hopefully – a happy home. In return they watch over us, help us with our work, protect us, entertain us, make us laugh, and... love us. They accept us as we are, and dispel our sadness with a wag of their tail. They enrich our lives with their presence. They give us the best thing they have to offer: themselves.

Dogs are extremely sensitive creatures who can detect and respond to the subtlest changes in our behaviour. On the whole, our lives with dogs and the relationships we have with them are well balanced and healthy.

But not all relationships between dogs and their owners are happy, healthy and enriching. Let's be realistic: dogs can also be aggressive, obstinate and scary. Sometimes they are difficult to understand. And old dogs in particular can sometimes exasperate us with their senile stubbornness. We humans are scatterbrained, ambivalent, and overworked. Dogs can push our buttons because they are such unambiguous, direct creatures, constantly expressing their needs and wants. If we find it hard to be authoritative and self-assured, if we are hesitant about taking the lead or are scared of losing control, then a dog makes it clear from day one who's in charge. Of course dogs *can* be heroic, wise, gentle and curative. But fundamentally they follow their own inclinations and their own code of conduct. And we do them a disservice if we romanticise them.

And unfortunately relationships aren't all golden sunsets – there are also dark thunderclouds to cope with. Violence comes in many forms. Everybody will have experienced or inflicted violence at some point in their lives. We can inflict violence on animals by hitting them, by failing to protect them, by walking out on them, by failing to set boundaries, or by utilising them for our own personal gain. These are all forms of violence and cruelty. And in particularly bad cases, violence against animals can be a first sign of psychological illness.

Do dogs really love us so much that we can do *anything* to them? Is a maltreated dog's love for its owner a real relationship, or a form of Stockholm syndrome, of a victim's sympathy for their abuser – as some critics label all human-dog relationships?[33]

What about my relationship with Shira? Isn't the word "no", which was almost a second name for her during her impetuous puppy years, a form of force? No matter how lovingly we treat our dogs, we will always have to put pressure on them at some point.

We can't let dogs live completely unconstrained lives. Without a collar and lead, they wouldn't survive very long on a busy road. For me, dog training was important in that it taught Shira the fundamental commands: sit, lie down, come here, stay. That ensured her safety in the world and my ability to take her anywhere. If that counts as using force, in the interests of her wellbeing and safety, then I plead guilty.

The fact is that few dogs these days can lead autonomous lives. While in the olden days they would have been on the move all day, trotting around the neighbourhood with their pals, today they are more frequently locked indoors. We make all their decisions for them: when and what they eat, when we go for a walk, and who they can play with. Dogs trade their freedom for safety. Whether they agree to that is not a question we can ask them. All this could be construed as violence, even if it is in their best interests.

So, do our dogs really love us unconditionally? Or is it actually more important to ask ourselves whether we love *them* unconditionally? Do we all love the dogs in our lives equally and in the same way? No. But that doesn't mean we don't love them all very, very much.

I don't expect Shira to love me and me alone. I am glad that she likes spending time with my parents and my friend Corina, and that my neighbours spoil her with treats. That doesn't diminish Shira's love for me. I want my dog to be happy, safe and healthy, wherever she is. Because that makes me happy too. When she comes over to me, puts her head in my lap and looks up at me, I don't care what her motive is. That alone is more than enough for me.

Konrad Lorenz once said, "Our wish to own a dog stems from the oldest desire of all – the longing of civilised human beings to return to a prelapsarian paradise."[34]

Perhaps we get a glimpse of paradise in the eyes of a dog.

You're Never Too Old
for New Tricks

························

"You can't teach an old dog new tricks." It's a saying that our parents rammed down our throats, to persuade us to finish our homework and try hard at school. But is it true?

Our general knowledge is definitely best when we're still young. I don't think I've ever known as much as I did when I finished school. We learn particularly quickly at that stage of life.

But I've enjoyed learning new things all my life, especially languages. I love travelling, and it's always a great feeling to make myself at least partially understood in a foreign country. That said, no matter how quickly I learn a new language, I forget it just as quickly if I don't practise. What's that lovely saying? "Use it or lose it." Nowadays I sometimes get into a flap if I can't remember something. Is it an early sign of dementia?

At a family party, I forgot what I was going to say and worked myself up into a real state about it. My nephew calmed me down: "Take it easy, Auntie, chill out. You just need to clear your head to make space for it."

He's right. There's too much going on in my brain. No wonder I can't fit any more in. The older I get, the more I try to cram into it, without ever stopping to have a clear out.

In actual fact, it is crucial for dogs to learn new things in their old age, because their day-to-day life changes completely. For instance, they have to come to terms with their physical limitations, needing to climb ramps and find their bearings despite their dwindling hearing and eyesight. We have to learn new ways of communicating with each other. So of course old dogs can learn new tricks, no matter what your parents told you. They might well have to take things more slowly, and you might need to bribe them with an extra biscuit. But as long as you're patient with them, it is perfectly possible.

It's not fair on our four-legged elders to stop setting them mental challenges. We teach young dogs an enormous amount, but when they get older, we stop asking anything of them. If we think we're doing them good by letting them enjoy the twilight of their lives in peace, we are mistaken. The same rule applies to dogs and humans alike: if you don't stay mentally active, sooner or later your brainpower will deteriorate. This is caused by a decline in the production of dopamine, a neurotransmitter responsible for motivation and memory. If people feel engaged and well balanced at an emotional level, dopamine is released in large doses – the reason why it is popularly referred to as the "happiness hormone".

So it makes sense to try and maintain high levels of dopamine in our old age, for the sake of our own wellbeing. To prove that this also applies to dogs, veterinary scientists from the University of Vienna developed a computer game adapted specially for them.[35] The principle is straightforward: the dogs solve puzzles by touching the screen with their muzzles, and they are rewarded with treats if they get it right. Just like a human taking up a new language or musical instrument in their old age, the dogs take many positives from learning new things and chalking up the victories. Constant brain training and problem solving generate positive emotional responses, slowing down the dogs' cognitive decline.

Of course, we don't need computer games to prove that learning new things together strengthens the bond between a dog and its owner. Learning brings dogs and humans happiness and enjoyment, no matter how old we are. It is a myth that "you can't teach an old dog new tricks".

And it's a real shame that the software and equipment used by the scientists in Vienna isn't yet available for domestic use. Software developers are currently being recruited to adapt the digital dog game for the household – but until then I'll just have to think up something else for Shira.

You can find plenty of books and online talks about how to keep old dogs busy. For labradors like Shira, anything to do with retrieving and scent tracking is a good start. Mantrailing is a particularly suitable activity for dogs who like following scents, as age and health are relatively unimportant. The dogs follow a human odour trail, picking up the scent from an object belonging to the person they are looking for and acclimatising to their individual smell. It works in any environment, on any surface: forest floor, grassy meadows, or even tarmac roads. Mantrailing also presents a challenge for the dog handler: they have to be able to "read" their dog during the search, seeing, interpreting, and reacting to every cue the creature gives them. These can be very subtle changes in body language, tail and head movement. Detecting and interpreting scents gives the dogs mental stimulation, nurturing and improving their concentration span enormously.

For old dogs, mantrailing is an ideal activity, even if they have orthopaedic problems, because musculoskeletal strain can be kept to a minimum. Ailments like hip dysplasia, spondylosis, arthritis, missing limbs and blindness are no obstacle to having some fun with scents. Another advantage of this type of workout is that the dogs work individually on a long lead, so they don't have to muck in with their fellow species. Even grumpy old codgers can work undisturbed.

When Shira was younger, I taught her lots of tricks that she can still do now. Sometimes my neighbours invite me to their children's parties – well, I suppose it's Shira who's really invited – and the children all love watching her perform her party pieces. Of course, it goes without saying that some of them don't work as well as they used to. Her hind legs are too weak to "dance" on anymore, but she can still sit up to beg, slalom through my legs, and fall over when I say "Peng!" The second trick also serves as part of Shira's physiotherapy. In addition, she still adores bringing me the post and taking the empty waste paper basket back to my desk. Presumably she agrees with Mahatma Gandhi: "Live as if you were to die tomorrow, and learn as if you were to live forever."[36]

My days of jogging through the woods with Shira are over; nowadays we take it slow. On one of our strolls, it struck me how much litter people drop in the woods. Leftovers in polystyrene containers, coffee cups, plastic bottles, cigarette butts – they are all just dumped on the ground by thoughtless people.

At some point I had the idea of bringing a bin bag on our walks and picking up other people's rubbish. Shira was on board straight away, and lent a helping paw. Since then, we've turned our favourite route into a regular eco mission. It's good practice for me: instead of stooping down to pick something up, I kneel down as my physiotherapist recommends. If I see some rubbish in an inaccessible spot or floating in the water, that's when Shira gets involved. I point her in the right direction, and she brings back anything that looks out of place to her. This not only keeps my old girl sharp between the ears, but also gives me the wonderful feeling of doing something good for the environment.

Old dogs and elderly humans too can learn new things their whole life long, and even outperform the youngsters in certain skills. For many of us, age can be an excuse for staying within our comfort zone: "I'm too old for that" becomes our catch-phrase. But we aren't too old in reality.

The neurologist Arne May at Hamburg-Eppendorf University Hospital carried out a series of fascinating studies on students and older people (between 50 and 67 years old).[37] He got them all to spend three months teaching themselves to juggle. People who could juggle already were not allowed to take part – so every participant was learning a completely new skill. And they all managed it. The older participants only needed a bit more time than the younger ones. The experts were stunned: up to that point, they had been convinced that brain matter stops increasing in adulthood. But Arne May believes new bonds can be formed and strengthened between pre-existing brain cells.

Having said that, the same area becomes depleted again if the subject stops practising the skill. Our brains are extremely flexible and can absorb new material, but lose it just as easily. For us, then, it really is a case of "use it or lose it". We need to keep challenging our brains to learn new things. It doesn't have to be juggling: perhaps you'd prefer a foreign language or painting. Or you could enrol as a mature student or observer at a university. I'm definitely still planning to learn the piano.

Naturally, the saying also holds true for physical exercise. Older people can at least partially work around their weaknesses by choosing a straightforward sport to play.

Many people continue to achieve amazing things at an advanced age. Galileo published his last book at 74. Goethe completed *Faust* when he was 80. Many artists, such as Mick Jagger, are still touring the world in their seventies, and continue to thrill fans with their music. It keeps them young and sprightly. Giuseppe Verdi was 77 years young when he started his opera *Falstaff*. Grandma Moses began her career as a painter in America after discovering her talent at well over 70 years old. The great German author Theodor Fontane only started writing novels at 60, and he didn't write his most famous works, such as *Effi Briest*, until a good while later. The legendary Charlie Chaplin never contemplated winding down. He had two more children at 70, and at 78 he wrote and directed his first and only colour film, *The Countess of Hong Kong*. Have I convinced you that your best years are still ahead of you?

Scared of trying new things? Dogs aren't. They are endlessly curious about life. One of my recent new year's resolutions was: "Break new ground". This year I've done many things that I had never done before, and I've learned a huge amount. That was just how I felt when I lived in the wild in a log cabin in Minnesota without electricity or running water. I had to learn to survive: chopping wood, cooking over a wood stove, angling and gutting fish, building a canoe, harvesting wild rice, and much more. For an amateur like me, it was all unimaginably difficult, but I have never felt as alive as I did then.

And I am always changing our routes for Shira's walks, to keep her daily life varied and engaging. Or we do the same old walks in reverse. It's astonishing how different familiar surroundings can suddenly look.

The incredible learning capacity of dogs is exemplified by Chaser, an American border collie who knows the names of 1,022 objects, and can even sort them into different categories (dummies, balls, frisbees).[38] Her owner, the psychologist John Pilley, who taught her all these words, called an end to the experiment after three years – not because Chaser couldn't learn any more, but because he himself had had enough and didn't want to spend the rest of his life teaching his dog new words. The human got bored of it; the dog didn't.

We learn a lot and gain a lot through intellectual curiosity. In his book about curiosity, Carl Naughton writes, "People who learn without enjoying themselves end up bitter. People who enjoy themselves without learning end up stupid."[39] His research asserts that curious people have up to 60% more fulfilling social relationships, and are more creative and conscientious in their work. And curiosity brings us back to our old friend the happiness hormone. If you are open to new experiences, your reward centre releases more happiness hormones. That is to say, curiosity and learning make us happy.

Choosing change. Being flexible. Leaving our comfort zone now and then. That's what makes us strong and happy. Learning new things can sometimes be really tiresome and time-consuming for us all – humans and dogs alike. But that's life. That's why Shira and I say: Forget your age, stay curious, keep moving, don't be scared to try new things, and have a good time.

Jump for Joy –
When You Can

Shira jumps about like a young dog and barks with excitement when I get her ball out of the car for a game of fetch. She wants to run, chase and play. I know that she'll be limping again come the evening – but there's no way she could just trot along slowly after a ball. I will give her a painkiller and ask her for forgiveness. Should I stop playing fetch with her just to spare her pain? When she's a dog with retrieving in her genes? No, I wouldn't have the heart for it. I know that limping is the price she and I have to pay for her happiness.

Even in her old age, Shira is still a ball junkie. I try to shorten our games, or at least slow them down. Instead of throwing the ball, I hide it and let her look for it. Scent work is easier on her joints.

In principle, play is a deliberate waste of time with no set goal. In our own lives, we're constantly talking about doing everything better, faster, more efficiently. We want to multitask, maintain inner balance, live in full flow, and juggle as many tasks as we can all at once. But at the moment it's more important for me to waste time, have fun with my old dog, and ignore the voice of my inner slave driver. Play warms my heart, as it does hers. What would our lives look like if we punctuated them with short bursts of unproductive, silly, wild and wonderful playtime? If we remembered that we're better off spending our lives loving, learning and laughing? And not scrambling around and making plans all the time? If we remembered that life is about enjoyment, not employment?

One day I'm out on a walk with Shira when I hear a man and a woman shouting animatedly, "Arko, coooome on, gooood boy, heeeere boy!" Curious, I head over for a closer look. An elderly couple are trying to persuade their dog to bring a dummy back. The two of them are hopping about like clowns, hollering in high-pitched voices, going down on their knees and opening their arms wide to try and catch Arko as he careers past them, nearly knocking them over in his feverish excitement. The old couple laugh out loud and laboriously help each other up again.

"He's 12 already – we got him from a rescue home," they tell me. "We hadn't been planning to get another dog at our age. But we just fell in love with him." Now they take him for a walk every day, which keeps them fit and healthy and is fun for them all.

Dogs let us become children again. A dog's enthusiasm for the slightest bit of fun is infectious. Whether it's a new toy, somebody at the door, or time for walkies, my Shira still gets excited even in her old age. She jumps up, wags her tail, and bounces around with delight.

Perhaps we should react similarly to events in our own lives. The next time you feel overwhelmed by your day-to-day life, stop for a moment and sniff some roses. Take a long, deep breath and do what a dog would do: if you catch a stranger's eye, beam at them and wish them a great day. Compliment an old lady on her hat. If a friend invites you for coffee, let them know how delighted you are. Don't hold back. Show your enthusiasm for the tiniest things, and have a good laugh at the baffled expressions you will be met with. You'll not only feel more relaxed, but you'll also begin to appreciate the beauty of your surroundings and take real pleasure in the simple things in life!

Animals spend the most time playing in the first few months of their lives, when their brains are developing rapidly. When they are older, they are not so reliant on constant stimulation. But their appetite for play and learning remains. The delight that dogs take in play should be an example to us. Taking pleasure in things enables us to learn more quickly and easily. Play not only gets us into shape physically, it also boosts creativity and open-mindedness. It is a necessary break from the daily grind. If we are constantly jumping from one thing to the next without taking any time out to recharge our batteries, we unsurprisingly get tired and burn out. It would be so much better for us to forget multitasking in favour of "multiplaying" – to bring more fun and games into our lives. Positive feelings, enjoyable group activities and shared experiences all bring us closer together. They let us know we can rely on each other.

But let's stay realistic: nowadays our dogs have fewer chances than ever to show off their zest for life and express their unbridled joy. Far too many people tell off their dogs for jumping up during a boisterous game, feel threatened by playful growling, or find it irritating if their dog gives their hand a friendly nudge on a walk. Certain types of behaviour are considered undesirable. Social constraints regarding showing consideration for one another put our dogs in corsets. Dogs are made to "behave", especially if they live in a city. This makes it all the more important for us to give them open spaces where they can be themselves and play together. People who get the opportunity to enjoy themselves cope better with stress. Humans and dogs who enjoy each other's company find their daily lives easier, and form closer bonds.

Have you ever seen a dog wheeling round in circles and jumping up and down because their owner is about to throw a ball or give them a biscuit? Wouldn't it be good if we could all skip around like that when there's something to be happy about? We live our lives at such a fast pace that we often forget to get excited about things or to celebrate good times, because we've already moved on to the next thing. We live in a wonderful world where the sun comes up every day, flowers bloom and the seasons change. There is a lot to jump for joy about.

Find something you like doing, and do it! I've never met a dog too busy to have fun. But I've met lots of people like that. Go outside or dance around the house when you're alone. Go crazy, and enjoy yourself! Life is too short not to play with the important people in our lives and have a good time.

Shira constantly reminds me to appreciate what's right in front of me. Now please excuse me – I'm off to play fetch.

Be Patient with Me, but Please Get On with It

It's a dark, blustery January morning, still quite early. Shira stirs, stands up and shakes herself. That's my cue to let her out. Normally I just open the door to the garden, but this time she goes to my wardrobe, where I keep her lead. That means she's got something bigger to do. I pull my jogging bottoms on over my pyjamas and slip into a light jacket, keeping my slippers on. That'll do for a quick stroll. When we come back, I'll have a couple of hours to write undisturbed. I grab Shira's lead, put her fluorescent collar on, and off we go to the big field at the edge of the woods.

"Hurry up, do a wee!" I chirp encouragingly to my deaf dog, letting her off the lead. But instead of squatting down straight away to do her business as usual, she wanders off serenely through the frosty grass.

The first drops of rain begin to fall, and the wind wrenches at my jacket. I haven't brought my umbrella with me, as I thought this would only be a short walk. The rain gets heavier and icier. I'm wet and tired, shivering from the cold. The windows of my warm house glow invitingly. But I stand firm, rooted to the spot, braving the elements.

Meanwhile, Shira seems to want to compensate for her hearing problems by thoroughly investigating every scent she picks up. Now, of all times! And so I stand there in the freezing rain, sold out by my old dog, who made me think she desperately needed to do her business, but actually just wanted to snuffle round every square centimetre of a great big field. No trace of guilty conscience or regret, no consideration whatsoever for her shivering owner.

Finally she squats down, does what she has to do, shakes a few raindrops off herself, and trots back to me, grinning and wagging her tail. "Lovely morning, isn't it? All done. Time to go home!"

Standing there in the miserable weather, I feel totally hacked off – but once again, I am spellbound by my dog. I love her for her stubbornness and peacefulness; I love how she does her own thing whatever the weather, refusing to let anything else get in her way. And yes, I envy her.

Those of us who live with old dogs learn to adjust the frenzied rhythm of our human lives to their slower pace. We realise we need to be patient when the end is drawing near.

For most people, time is money. But the world doesn't work to our timetable – it has its own natural rhythms. Why should I force my dog to do something she's not ready to do? Anyone who has waited in the pouring rain for a dog to do its business knows what I'm talking about. I work to Shira's schedule.

What does patience mean in the modern world? I feel like I'm always at the back of the queue. When I finally get to the till at the supermarket, the cashier inevitably runs out of receipts or the old lady in front of me starts laboriously emptying out her purse to count out her change. In motorway traffic jams, the cars in the next lane always seem to be moving forward more quickly than me. And the trains are always delayed. We've unlearned how to wait. Too much in today's world is only a mouse click away. For my research, I no longer have to trawl through books in a library or loan them out. I just go online. Back in the day, I would have spent weeks waiting for a parcel – now I order from a large mail order company in the morning, and it's delivered the next day. We are used to having everything go to plan. If it doesn't, we get impatient. Waiting stresses us out.

When I'm working on a book project, or worse, when I've got a pressing deadline for a manuscript, the only thing that matters to me is completing it in time. My mind is buzzing day and night. I stop seeing what's happening around me. And eventually I can't take it anymore. My brain is empty all of a sudden. I begin to panic, doubting I'll ever be able to scale the enormous mountain looming up before me. I worry that I will lose my creativity. And I long for nothing more than a desert island to escape to for the next six months.

Then I see Shira rolling onto her back enthusiastically, kicking her legs in the air, content with herself and the world around her. I envy her. Why can't *I* be like that? Why does everything have to happen to me all at once, with so little warning? Why do I put myself under so much pressure?

My old girl shows me how it's done every single day. Where she used to be an absolute maniac with no off button, she now lies peacefully in the sun, watching the world go by. She's turned off the fast lane of life and into a quiet side road. There is an enviable languor to her existence. My old dog seems to live by the Japanese proverb, "If you're in a hurry, slow down. If you're in a real hurry, take a detour."

I try to be like her. Instead of waiting impatiently for her to finish shaking hands with every blade of grass and sniffing every flower from top to bottom, I stand there, taking a closer look at what goes on in her world. The grass is damp with rain, dew sparkling in the morning sun. A bird is sitting on a branch, singing a song – the sound of spring. The first cranes fly over the landscape, blaring loudly. I feel the warm sun on my face. Shira has finished snuffling about. She's looking for me. This time I haven't hurried on ahead like I've done often enough – I'm still here. We smile at each other. Silent understanding: life is beautiful.

My manuscripts and deadlines pale into insignificance. The rush of everyday life vanishes for a moment. The gift of patience brings my hectic activities to a standstill, just for a little while.

On a book tour in a busy city, I took some time out and went for a wander in the park, where I caught sight of a man walking his dog. The man had infinite patience. The dog "read the newspaper" from beginning to end, snuffled around here and there, took a few tentative steps into the little pond, sat down and had a look around. The owner didn't mind at all.

In perfect contrast with this pair, a man in a suit then strode past, pulling his dog along behind him, typing hastily on his smartphone and occasionally shouting angry commands at the creature behind him. The dog appeared to be nothing but an irritating accessory. The man might as well have been dragging just the lead and collar behind him – without the dog. Sometimes I want to grab people by the shoulders and give them a good shake. "Can't you see what you're doing?" But they probably wouldn't understand.

We're always in a hurry. Feeling pressed for time has become a dominant feature of our lives. The pace of our world has quickened, and many people feel rushed off their feet and powerless against the inexorable march of time. We utilise every spare minute to cram more and more into each day. Takeaway coffee here, speed-training workout there. With every technical innovation designed to make our lives easier, we turn up the heat more and more. For many of us, doing nothing means wasting time. We can't handle inactivity.

Dogs let us discover the moments in our lives when the world stands still. The time I spend with my old dog helps me reflect on the next few hours or the coming week, and concentrate on taking it slow. I step back from the demands of our lightning-fast world. I float away to a little island and feel enormously grateful for that single moment of calm.

Time – how meaningless it is in the wider context of our universe. This thought occurred to me when I went to a European Space Agency exhibition at the Hessisches Landesmuseum in Darmstadt about Rosetta, the comet-hunting space probe. Space travel and the universe have always fascinated me. On seeing the probe, I felt I had finally grasped the elusive concept of time. I compared Rosetta's journey with Shira's life.

In March 2004, an Ariane rocket launched the probe into space to investigate the origins of our solar system. At this point Shira wasn't around yet; she was only born the following year. In November 2014, 10 and a half years later, a lander, Philae, detached from the probe and touched down on the comet 67P/Churyumov-Gerasimenko. In September 2016, Rosetta also landed on this comet, completing its assignment. By the end of this ESA mission, Shira was a golden oldie. Rosetta had covered seven billion kilometres in the course of her short life.

These sorts of figures transform a dog's life into the blink of an eye. It is humbling to know how infinite our universe is and how old our planet is, and it makes me even more grateful that I am able to share my short time on earth with my dog. What an unbelievably wonderful "accident" it is that the two of us found each other in this life!

Embrace Silence

Shira is lying in the grass. The sun is shining; it's too hot for us both. As I watch her sleeping, tears prickle my eyes. Why is the painful thought of losing her occurring to me now, of all times? I find it even sadder to think about what *she's* already lost. She can't run through the fields as quickly as she used to, and hour-long walks are history. But what makes me think she's sad about that too? Where did I get this idea that she should be upset by the change in her abilities? How well do I really know Shira after all?

We think we know our dogs, that we can "read" them. Life with them is one long process of interpretation that takes years to refine. We develop our own "language" to communicate with each other. We talk to our dogs our whole lives long – sometimes more than we do to our two-legged friends. We can't communicate with animals over WhatsApp or Facebook: we rely on talking face to face.

We assume that dogs only react to our tone of voice (high voice for praise, deep voice for tickings-off) and that it doesn't matter what we say. But watch out! A new study shows that they also react to the content of sentences.[40] So if I said something mean to Shira in a cutesy voice, she would notice and take exception to it.

Perhaps it's just my demeanour that betrays me, because dogs are predominantly guided by our body language and facial expressions. Hearing plays a lesser role in human-dog relationships. And anyway, since Shira went deaf, I haven't been able to use words or sounds for communication or commands. "Shiiiiira, heeeeere" doesn't work anymore. She simply can't hear me. So now I "talk" with hand gestures instead. At a distance, I signal "heeeeere" by standing bolt upright with my legs spread and arms out wide. At close quarters, I beckon her by patting my thighs or waving her towards me. When I do my Come-Here-For-A-Cuddle signal, crouching down and opening my arms wide, her eyes light up and she runs grinning towards me at full geriatric speed. "Stay" is an outstretched arm with my palm turned out towards her. To get her to lie down, I put my hand flat on the floor, and "sit" is a raised index finger. That used to be the signal for her to bark, so it can happen that when I command her to sit, she barks in response. But what does it matter? We'll get there eventually.

For practical purposes, I use a long lead or a Flexi lead in places where I can't let her off. In the dark I signal to her with a torch or a laser pointer if I want something from her. If she's fast asleep and I need to wake her up, I have to take care not to give her a fright. I stomp about the room like an elephant so that she'll feel the vibrations in the floor, or wave something about in the air to create a "breeze". Only then do I touch her. Once when I stroked her without warning, she was scared witless and literally jumped into the air. Some dog owners tell me their dogs can bite if they are busy snuffling around on a walk and an unfamiliar dog – or person – touches them unexpectedly. That's why I'm always wary when other people (and dogs) cross paths with Shira, and I do my best to prevent any misunderstandings in advance. Instead of "She doesn't bite," I shout from afar, "She can't hear you!"

I know Shira's body language better than ever, and I also have to take care to get my own right. It's easier to work on my own body language than it is to try and change my dog's nature. Shira forces me to send clear messages. She doesn't want me to make tentative suggestions, she doesn't want anything to be up for discussion. She expects clarity and calmness in my gestures – she wants to know where she stands. Only then does she feel safe. If I leave the house and my old girl's still asleep, I make my presence felt so that she notices I'm going. Otherwise she might wake up and think I've abandoned her. I don't want to put her through that.

Communicating with my deaf dog has also taught me to express myself more clearly in my day-to-day life. No more umming and ahing, but simple, straightforward statements. It's astonishing how easy it is if you just try it.

I have also learned to behave differently around humans with hearing difficulties. Yes, it's a pain in the neck if someone can't understand what you're trying to tell them. But how do we react? We bellow at them, or we just declare that "they can't hear a thing" and give up talking to them. What if we treated them the same way we would treat a deaf dog? We would stand close to them, perhaps touching their arm to get their attention. We wouldn't turn away while speaking to them, but look them in the eye and speak clearly. We don't have to shout at people with hearing difficulties, and we don't have to dumb down our language for them. They're deaf, not stupid.

I once learned how beneficial it is to have a break from talking (and listening) at a seminar on the topic of "religion and animals". The seminar was held in the house of silence at Königsmünster Abbey, in the Ruhr valley. We were allowed to speak in the seminar rooms, but had to remain silent at mealtimes and everywhere else in the building.

It was my first time at a silent retreat, and it felt very strange. At the start, I was even a little uncomfortable. No polite conversation at the table. A nod of the head to say hello, a smile of thanks when someone passed the bread or salt. I was suddenly confronted with my own reflection. No distractions now. After a few days I began to relax, to listen to my body, and to develop a more conscious appreciation for the world around me. Silence gives our thoughts, memories and feelings a chance to come back where they belong. Silence transforms you as a person.

Afterwards, I tried practising silence outside the abbey as well. When signing for a package, I gave the delivery driver a silent smile, and nodded to the cashier at the supermarket without saying anything. I found it astonishing that no one noticed I hadn't said a word. Everyone else was so busy talking that my silence was simply drowned out. Our society is talk, talk, talk. Life in a house of silence seems extreme nowadays, but it's not as extreme as non-stop talking. Non-stop. All the time! To communicate, to inform, to divert, to lie, to fill time. We escape the intensity of silence by talking. But silence can give you the chance to recuperate. Silence stops us putting on an act, and lets us be ourselves. It lets us relax.

Is that how Shira feels now that she's deaf? She probably doesn't really mind. Unlike humans, who attach so much importance to language and tone of voice, she has no problem understanding and communicating with her fellow dogs. So comparing her with a deaf person doesn't really work. And her deafness does have its advantages. Shira sleeps much more deeply now. Because she's free of aural distractions, she responds better to my body language when learning new tricks. Her poor hearing indisputably helps her concentration, unlike other dogs, who have to block out street noise, barking and other external influences.

Our old dogs are in love with life – whether it's noisy or quiet outside. They don't get cast down by the symptoms of old age. So why should we?

Trust Your Instincts

Now and then someone comes into our lives and leaves a particularly lasting mark. For me, that was Lady. From the moment I first held her in my arms until the day she died, she was the light and love of my life. I have loved many dogs in my time, but if every human being has a canine soulmate, mine was Lady.

I was living in the USA when I met her, the day before she was due to die. A deafening chorus of barking engulfed me as I opened the door to the dog enclosure at the animal shelter in Virginia Beach. I was in a large room lined with two rows of cages, one on top of the other. In each cage was a dog, most of them barking their heads off. They had good reason to, because I was in a "kill shelter", a facility where animals who aren't adopted after a certain length of time are put to sleep. This is common practice in the USA, to save money and contain the deluge of "unwanted" animals that shelters receive. Three million animals are put to sleep each year because nobody wants them.

I had gone there to hand in a stack of old papers and a crate of empty bottles for a friend, as the animal shelter recycled them for money. But then I cast a look around the room full of dogs, and I saw her…

The frightened little labrador was cowering in the far corner of her cage in the upper row, looking at me with pleading intensity in her big brown eyes, as though imploring me to help her.

"You're here! Finally, you're here! Where have you been all this time?"

I think our souls had been knit together long before we met face to face.

The only other thing in her cage was a blanket. One of the staff appeared at my side straight away.

"That's Lady," she said. "She's being put to sleep tomorrow."

"What? Why? She's such a beautiful dog," I replied.

"She was actually due to have the injection last week. But we kept her a bit longer, because we couldn't believe no one would take such a lovely pup."

The staff member told me the dog had been handed in because her owner (who had one other dog) had become homeless and couldn't afford to feed two dogs anymore. Because she was freezing cold and still very fragile at only eight months old, the employees had put a blanket in her cage. I went up to the grille and gazed into her brown eyes. Then Lady came over to me and cautiously licked my fingers.

At that moment, the dark cage lit up, as if a ray of sun had suddenly burst through a cloud. "I'll be back," I promised. "And after that, I'll never let you out of my sight."

"Kismet" is a word from Arabic culture that means "a person's fate as determined by Allah", or "an inevitable destiny". This was kismet: I had left my behavioural research placement a week earlier than planned, for no particular reason, and headed to Virginia to visit a friend the very same week that Lady had been spared the lethal injection by a kindly rescue worker – before I then turned up carrying papers and bottles at the crucial moment.

Rescuing a dog from an animal shelter is always a bureaucratic nightmare, no matter where in the world you are. Although the only alternative for Lady was death, the animal shelter regulations didn't make it at all easy for me to adopt her. Before they handed her over, she had to be spayed. Then they had to carry out a location check to ensure she was going to a good home. Well, I could hardly summon the inspectors to Germany, could I? Fortunately, a friend jumped in who had previously adopted several animals from the same shelter. She vouched for me, telling them how happy Lady would be with me. The shelter staff didn't quite break the rules, but they bent them to the limit for us. Though I had to wait several days for the green light, I felt confident.

And I mean it: there's a reason all these "coincidences" brought me and Lady together. We trusted that it would work out, and trust became the foundation of our long and happy relationship.

Before we flew home, Lady and I travelled around the USA for half a year and got to know each other better. But back in Germany, things were less straightforward, as I was going through a very difficult time personally. My life was chaotic by both human and dog standards. Lady and I had to deal with several house moves, as well as a painful break-up. The only constant in my life was my dog's love. She didn't enjoy that period of change, but we were sure everything would be alright in the end.

At some point in our lives, we all learn that it's good to let go and to have faith in the future. Lady showed me that trust can continue to build until it is as unconditional as love.

Without trust – in ourselves and in others – we can't survive. If I were constantly questioning whether I was a good dog owner or not, I wouldn't be any good because I'd be so busy worrying about it. So I simply do my best and trust that

that will be good enough. Trust breeds strength and support, providing security and companionship in our lives.

We have a good life in Europe. We live in rich, safe countries. But we distrust everybody. When I lived in the wild in Minnesota, we never locked the log cabin, not even when we went on holiday. "What if someone has an emergency and needs help?" my boyfriend said. If they did, it would be a relief to find an unlocked cabin for shelter. We trusted people.

Trust is a necessary component of life. We drive to work trusting that our headlights will keep working. We trust that the structural engineers did their job properly when building our house and that the ceiling won't fall in. We trust our doctor's diagnosis. If we didn't do all of this, we'd be completely incapable of anything.

To put your trust in someone, you need the courage to open up and make yourself vulnerable. I've been a trusting person all my life – and have fallen flat on my face more than enough times. At some point, I started to reduce the number of people I opened up to, so as to avoid being hurt. I preferred to keep my own company and to keep everything under control. But control is an illusion. Who can say for certain that they've never been lied to or betrayed? I learned from Lady, and Shira too, that it is okay to trust the people close to us. Even when it could mean getting hurt. Life is like that sometimes.

I really didn't have anything to worry about in this respect. The social psychologist David Dunning, from Cornell

University in Ithaca, New York, conducted a series of trust experiments with students that proved more than 80% of the population is absolutely trustworthy.[41] Eight out of ten strangers paid back money that someone had lent them – even when they could have kept the sum without punishment. The results were identical everywhere – in the USA, the Netherlands, and Germany.

Another current survey shows that almost every other person would lend financial support to interesting projects via crowdfunding.[42] Crowdfunding is a way of getting projects, products, start-ups and lots more off the ground. What's unusual about it is that it relies on support from a large number of people. It is founded on trust.

It is no coincidence that experts talk about trust in the context of "social capital". Trust is the reason why children can play carefree in the neighbourhood, and why business-people can close deals with a handshake alone. Trust makes everyday life easier, without a shadow of doubt.

It makes us happier too, because if we assume other people have good intentions from the start, we don't treat them with suspicion, and we're rewarded for it. Most of the time, at least. Trust is a feeling that defies complete control.

Dogs understand what goes on beneath the surface. They rely on their gut feelings. We experience similar feelings, but many of us ignore our own instincts or suppress them altogether. I always try to trust my instincts. If I have a bad feeling in my stomach, if I feel uncomfortable in certain situations, then I can't trust the outcome.

One example is when I'm hiring someone for work around the house. I pay attention to how they behave around Shira, observing how my dog reacts to them. If she trots over happily with a toy in her mouth and lets them stroke her, I give them the job. If Shira keeps her distance and is cautious around them, the deal's dead. I trust my dog's instincts around people I don't know.

Do they feel the same about us?

Our dogs trust us blindly – even more so the older they get. When Shira was a puppy, it was a while before she rolled onto her back and exposed her bare stomach for me to tickle. Trust takes time. Today the two of us trust each other unconditionally. If Shira is lying calmly on her side, I kneel down next to her and stroke her back, gently massaging the spot low down on her spine which always makes her roll onto her back with pleasure. Then I tickle her stomach. Our bond moves me, and I pray that I deserve her trust and that I can always be the person she thinks I am.

Things Aren't Important

Life is complicated – from filling out tax returns, to design-ing websites, to programming the TV to record your favourite show. But these are all material problems. Compared to us, dogs are refreshingly frugal. They have very few needs and wants. When I'm with Shira, I rediscover my sense of perspective. She reminds me of the important things in life, the things we can enjoy together.

"Simplicity is the fruit of maturity," according to Friedrich Schiller.[43] And how right he is. When we are young, we accumulate possessions that we'll want to get rid of again when we're older. In our old age, we're probably readier to let go of items that aren't important to us anymore, because we know we can't take anything with us when we die. My grandmother always said, "The final shirt has no pockets." Every surplus bit of "stuff" is a burden.

I recently started experimenting with minimalism for the first time. I stopped consuming more than necessary, and began to clear out my house bit by bit. In Sweden, they have a particular word for this: "Döstädning", which essentially means "tidying up in case I die", so that nobody has to wrestle with all my stuff when I'm not around anymore. What a brilliant idea. The Swedish author Margareta Magnusson wrote a book on it entitled *The Gentle Art of Swedish Death Cleaning*.[44] The 80-year-old takes the view that "the fewer things you have, the more time you have to live". It's not just about getting rid of things, it's also about taking responsibility – for other people and for future generations. One of her most important discoveries was that "letting go of things, people and pets when there's nowhere else to turn is a hard lesson to learn. But the longer I live, the more I have to come to terms with it." The book absolutely fascinated me, helping me to clear out my house (and my life). And even my dog has benefitted from this new simplicity: since I can now concentrate more on the essentials, I am noticeably less stressed and distracted, and have more time for her.

If we clutter our surroundings, we start to feel like we're drowning in work. Our lives come apart at the seams, and it all becomes too much. It's important to give some structure to our belongings, and to our lives as a whole. Tidying up helps, because it makes us think about what we really want or need.

I dress plainly. Fashion just isn't my thing. For dog walks, jeans and a sweatshirt are all I need. If I didn't have to go to the occasional lecture, I'd be going around in a tracksuit all the time. While I've been sorting out my flat, it has struck me how much better I feel when things are clear and tidy. The fewer things I possess, the more I can concentrate on the really important things in life.

I've started giving away all my clothes and belongings that I haven't worn or used in over two years. I've even given away many of my beloved books, only holding on to the ones that are particularly important to me or that I want to read again, which has created some space on my shelves. I use an eReader on my travels. But the most important thing of all is to limit the amount I consume. For every new thing I buy, an old one has to go.

I have dragged my dog into my minimalist crusade, clearing out her large toy box. The number of cuddly toys has reduced dramatically, and my neighbours' dogs were delighted to have the things she stopped playing with a long time ago. No, I'm not depriving my "poor old dog". There are still enough toys lying about for someone to trip over. I've washed the rest of them and stored them away in the cellar. Now and then I bring up a "new" toy for Shira, and she's happy as Larry. Does she know it's a trick?

It's liberating to know how little we really need. Now Shira and I can delight even more in life's simple pleasures: sitting in the sun, being in nature, walking and swimming.

The more chaotic and hectic our lives seem to be, the more we long for simplicity within ourselves, in our hearts and minds. At that point, we must acknowledge that getting rid of our possessions and living a minimalist life will give us more space not only physically, but also mentally.

The American comedian Will Rogers once said, "Too many people spend money they haven't earned, to buy things they don't want, to impress people they don't like."[45]

I don't attach any importance to fashion – human or canine. Shira currently has three collars (one for day-to-day life, one "official" one for her TV appearances, and one fluorescent one), one bowl, and four leads (a light lead that fits in my jacket pocket, a Flexi lead for long walks, her predecessor's old lead, and a long lead that I bought her as a puppy).

In addition, my old girl has two coats for the cold seasons: one fleece and one waterproof jacket. I went to great expense without batting an eyelid to buy her beds. While my own furniture comes from a certain Swedish furniture store, Shira has several luxury orthopaedic mattresses, designed to ease the strain on her joints – at least one in every room. I didn't buy these so Shira could go bragging to her pals. I admit that she doesn't really need it all, and would still be happy with a blanket on the floor and a chewed-up old ball, but it helps make my old dog's everyday life easier (and mine too). Appearances aren't important, but quality and functionality are.

Of course you do see dogs with collars and leads in every colour and material, as well as coats and jumpers to match their owners' outfits. But animals don't care about their appearance. Dogs prefer to go around "naked" – or soaked to the skin, in the case of my labrador. Dog fashion says more about the owner than the dog.

For Shira, happiness is having her tummy stroked, going for a walk in the sun (or the rain), and getting a treat or a kind word when she isn't expecting it. She takes pleasure in the simplest things, and lives to love and be loved. What's important isn't the length of a walk, but the very idea of doing something together. When we sit down to rest on a hillside after a walk and look out over the landscape together, her eyes gleam with delight as she leans into me. "Thanks for a great day!"

Live in the Present

The weather forecast is predicting another hot summer's day, so Shira and I go for a big walk at crack of dawn. We'll want to spend the rest of the day relaxing in the shade. I've brought a thermos of tea and some sandwiches – it's breakfast in the woods today. Shira's on good form. She runs off ahead, tracking scents, checking the messages left by other dogs and leaving the occasional reply. Then she throws herself onto her back in the dewy grass, her legs kicking and floundering in the air like a beetle. We sit down for breakfast in a clearing on the edge of the woods, nestling together on a rug, enjoying the sunrise and the birdsong. Life is great.

A few metres from us, a deer takes a few tentative steps out of the woods, grazing peacefully. I nudge my old girl, directing her attention to the deer. She glances up at me, then at the deer, sighs "Lovely!" and lays her head back down on her forepaws. A few years ago, I would have had to restrain her from launching herself after any potential prey, but now she only follows it with her eyes.

The first rays of sun strike Shira's fur, enveloping her in a golden light. And right in the middle of this wonderful moment, the same unsolicited thoughts surge within me once more. I ask myself how much time the two of us have left.

Shira raises her head and looks at me. "I'm still here," I hear her say. "I'm still alive. Stop thinking about the future. *Carpe diem!*"

I realise with astonishment that my dog is quoting the Roman poet Horace.

"Seize the day." She grins. "You think he thought of that first?"

I laugh out loud, and the deer sprints away in fright.

"You're right. If anyone coined that phrase, it was you animals. You've been doing it for thousands of years."

Carpe diem! Shira has – yet again – reminded me to be more like her. Far too often I put myself under pressure, and when it all gets too much, my body responds, and I go down with back pains or a cold. I have to draw the line somewhere and take better care of myself.

Shira is my "first aid officer". When I'm mentally exhausted, she realises before I do, and lets me know it's high time for a walk. So I take her out to the woods. For the first half hour, my thoughts are usually still flying around uncontrollably in my head, but little by little I force myself to turn my attention to my dallying old dog. I watch her snuffling over the ground, deep in concentration. I hear a squirrel grunting and try to catch a glimpse of the ravens croaking in the treetops. And eventually I manage to escape my own thoughts and find freedom for a moment.

If Shira designed a calendar, on every page she'd just write "NOW" across the top. Because that's all that counts for her. "Later" is a word she doesn't understand. Although she's slowing down in her old age, she isn't worried about gaining weight or doing more exercise. She's enviably indifferent to all that.

Dogs have the gift of concentrating fully on what's important to them in the moment. For my labrador, that's usually food. Shira knows where our neighbours keep their tin of dog biscuits in the kitchen, and makes a beeline for it the moment she's through the front door. She dashes to the cupboard containing the treats, asks politely for her share, and lies down contentedly afterwards. The biscuits are in the past, the future is unknown. The only thing that counts is the present.

While I sometimes drift through the days, fiddling with my emails or the internet, Shira concentrates fully on *one* thing at a time. I admire how she focuses her energies, inspiring me to copy her and concentrate properly on the task in front of me.

Dogs live in the here and now. Not in the five minutes just gone, not in the future. In the present. They can make their favourite ball the centre of the universe, but a few seconds after it rolls away, they forget it was ever there, and turn to something else. Why? Because dogs don't live in their heads. We humans are constantly miles away, wrapped up in our wandering thoughts, reliving the past or fantasising about what is still to come. Dogs, meanwhile, are happy where they are – they never want to be anywhere else. They don't daydream about chasing a frisbee on the beach when they're hunting squirrels in the woods. A dog just IS. Dogs interact with the world fully and directly.

Some dogs can't get enough of cars. They love sticking their head out of the window, sniffing the air and feeling the wind in their fur. They don't care where they're going. They're just enjoying the ride. We should do the same. Sure, we set ourselves admirable goals, but all too often we forget that what matters is how we get there. If we concentrate too hard on the outcome and our rigid expectations are not fulfilled, we end up frustrated, depressed, or even angry. So, the next time you set yourself a target, keep yourself open to other possibilities, enjoy every moment of excitement and creativity, have fun, and learn from the journey you are undertaking. You don't need to stick your head out of the car window to make it happen, but do treasure the fresh air and the new scents that greet you as you set out on your next adventure.

Many dog owners have written to me describing how happy caring for their old or sick dogs makes them – no matter how difficult and tedious it is. They do it without thinking, and their pet rewards them with deepest gratitude. Take Christine, whose Pomeranian Benny made it to 15, but had a tough time in the second half of his life. Alongside a heart condition, Benny was diagnosed with spondylosis, gastritis, and several secondary illnesses. Christine's life became dominated by her dog's health. She told me:

"When Benny was in a good way, my family and I were too. Although our little one had so many issues, his eyes still lit up and radiated joy when he felt good. And I was prepared to do anything for him – that was what made me happy. We spent lots of time cuddling and snuggling. I just went with it. Thinking back, I'm so happy I did. My little one craved physical contact with his family, and of course we all gladly provided it. Benny taught us not to strive for happiness, but to enjoy the nice things the present has to offer and to stick it out in hard times. A dog demands so little and gives so much. While we were looking after our old boy, we lost a few human friends, because we declined several invitations so as to save Benny unnecessary exertion. It was out of the question for us to leave him alone for hours at a time. Today we're glad that we chose him. Although it was enormously painful to come to terms with the fact the little guy's time was slowly running out, it also taught us a very valuable lesson. We lived every day as if it was the last. That period taught us to live more deliberately. I didn't want to miss a second, not even the hours and days of constant worry."

Many people who live with an old dog only realise the clock is ticking towards the end of their time together. They suddenly feel a sharp pang of longing, and realise they are missing something. They're unhappy. They have the wrong job, live in the wrong place, or are in the wrong relationship. Our dogs' old age can be a useful opportunity to reflect on our own lives. But let's not forget to concentrate on the present. Because you don't find happiness by measuring the present against the future or the past – you can only find it if you let your heart settle into the here and now, as people try to do through pilgrimages or challenging meditation exercises.

This morning, as I tickle Shira's warm tummy in the sunshine, my heart fills with joy in the present moment.

Dogs show us that the present is of utmost importance. We can't change yesterday or tomorrow, but we can love our families, children and friends right now, with our whole hearts. Look at how happy dogs are when they are living a well-balanced life. For a dog, a balanced lifestyle isn't a big ask: a daily routine of movement, good food, and plenty of sleep. It's not that hard, is it? It certainly shouldn't be too much for us.

Although her haunches hurt, Shira greets me like a returning hero every time I come back from somewhere, no matter how long I've been gone. She jumps off the sofa and skids across the floor, waggling her tail like a propeller. Her favourite occupation is being with me. When we realise how few dog years we have left, we want every loving moment to feel like it'll last forever. But the present is all we have – so let's fill it with love.

Unfortunately, our dogs never live long enough. I've already outlived two dogs, and by all estimates I'll outlive Shira too. I'm scared of saying goodbye, and try to shut the idea out of my mind. I want to concentrate on the final portion of our life together, and to enjoy it.

The American author and preacher Henry Ward Beecher once said, "We spend so much time on things that are urgent that we have none left to spend on those that are important." It doesn't matter if it's urgent – if it's not important, we shouldn't be doing it.

For dogs, every single day is important and exciting. They wait for us to come home, relish the opportunity to say hello to a visitor, and are thrilled when we pick up their lead, because it means walkies. We can learn so much just by observing how they make the most of the simple pleasures in life.

The Wisdom of Old Dogs

For Shira, every day is an adventure that is still to be revealed. Now, in her old age, we have walked the same old routes countless times. But she never seems to get bored of them. She delights in the wonders of the world around her, the breeze blowing from a different direction, carrying new scents. Life offers her countless possibilities, and she makes the most of them all. Life is waiting for us to discover it.

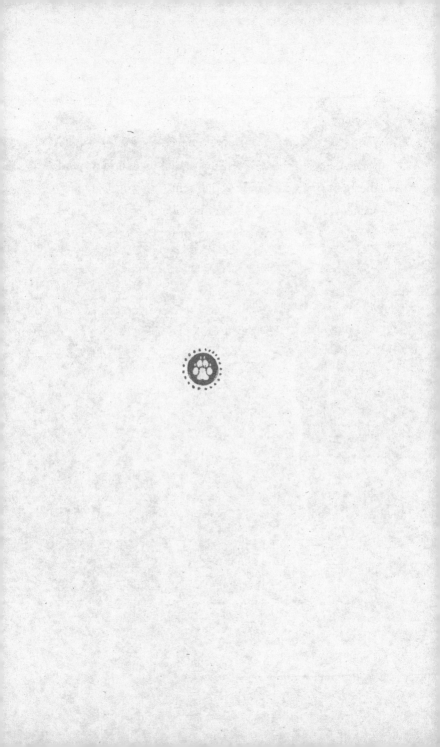

Every Day
is a Gift

Holiday! Finally! After months of work on my new book, I'm ready to run away to a desert island – or the seaside at the very least. I've promised my Shira a holiday in Denmark. She was born there, on the small island of Mandø in the Wadden Sea. I want to take my old girl back home again. I know it's sentimental of me. She probably doesn't mind where we go – as long as there's water, which is of primal importance to a labrador. But for her, the most important thing is just to be with me.

I've rented a cottage in Henne Strand, tucked away behind the dunes. The only sounds are the breaking waves and the occasional call of a pheasant. In the mornings a young fallow deer stalks through the heather, and dune rabbits hop past my window. Shira sleeps through it all.

April is the perfect time for a holiday. We got up early this morning for a stroll over the dunes to the beach. Walking through sand is hard work for my old dog. But the moment she sees the sea, that's all forgotten. Her labrador genes take over and she races towards the water as fast as her old legs will carry her. In she goes with an almighty splash!

I don't know if she knows where she is – if this holiday actually is a sort of homecoming for her. But it's certainly satisfying her love of water. She sploshes along the shore and jumps head first into the waves. She never goes out too far, fortunately, as I'm worried the current might sweep her out to sea and she wouldn't be strong enough to swim back.

After our morning walk we head out along Henne Mølle, a strip of fresh water that runs into the sea. The current is much weaker here, and Shira works up the courage to swim upstream, taking occasional big gulps of water. Swimming is a great alternative to the physio exercises she does at home. I can't help smiling as I watch her climbing clumsily up out of the water onto the sandbank, a cheerful grin on her face: "Water! It's the best!"

Each morning on our way back towards the cottage, we meet up with some elderly friends, human and canine – other holidaymakers who come here with their old dogs to savour the stillness of the broad, empty beach. There's Ilka from Norway and her 16-year-old crossbreed, a Danish man and his grey (formerly black) fluffy poodle, and me and Shira. All our dogs are deaf. The three of us communicate in a mishmash of three languages and hand gestures. We wander along the path together, letting our grey-muzzled companions set the pace, before all going our separate ways. I am struck by the calm, contentment and happiness radiating from the other dog owners. They are simply happy to be on holiday, and grateful for the opportunity to take good care of their old dogs. Owners of old dogs exude humility and grace.

Back at the cottage, I make myself a coffee and settle down on the terrace with a book. Shira stretches out on her blanket in the sun. Droplets of water glisten like diamonds on her fur. She breathes deeply and calmly.

Suddenly we both look up at the same time and gaze over at the waves breaking on the beach. As if on command, we turn to look at each other.

"Do you remember?" I ask Shira.

"Mm."

I want to ask her something meaningful: if she remembers her last holiday here with me, or her puppyhood. What does it mean to her to be back here with me? But we don't need deep and meaningful declarations to validate the bond we share. Our bond will never fade.

We both let out a deep breath and turn back to what we were doing. I go back to my book, while Shira rests her head on her forepaws and goes back to sleep.

When I wake up, the sun is hanging low in the sky. Sleep and fresh air have done me good, helping me forget the stressful journey. I stand up and stretch. Shira sits up and looks at me excitedly. Her tail wags from side to side.

"Hi, my love. Fancy a stroll down to the *water*?"

Her favourite word. My old dog jumps up.

"Alright then, let's go!" I pick up her lead and we set off through the dunes towards the beach. I motion towards the sea, and she sprints off ahead. Before she plunges into the surf, Shira runs two great big circles around the beach for sheer joy, glances back at me one last time, and then there's no more holding back. I take my shoes off, roll up my trouser legs and run into the water behind her.

Here we are on holiday together once more, savouring every minute. Sitting on the dunes, side by side, swathed in the scent of the ocean. The phrase "once more" has come to define everything I do. I know what the future holds in store. The thought that this might be our last holiday together can get me down, but mostly it just makes me feel incredibly fortunate. This holiday is a gift for us both. All these wonderful experiences that we can't hold onto − all too soon they will simply be fleeting memories. But even after we return home to our daily routine, this week will continue to nourish us for a long time to come. Above all, our holidays give us another opportunity to grow together, as our bond becomes stronger and the time we have left becomes more and more precious. And that is another reason to be thankful.

Sometimes I am kept awake by thousands of thoughts whirling around my head. I toss and turn, trying to clear my mind. Nothing doing. Eventually I settle down, lie still in bed, and listen to Shira's deep snoring. I'm scared of the time in the not-too-distant future when that comforting sound will give way to silence. Letting the gentle sound of her breathing engulf me, I settle into its rhythm, and finally slip into dreamland. My last thought is one of simple gratitude.

I am an extremely early riser, and my old dog has adapted to it. At five o'clock on the dot she gets up out of her cosy bed, stretches, and shakes herself. That's my cue to let her outside. Shira trudges sleepily out of the door. On the way to the back of the garden, she stops and looks towards the kitchen window, where I'm busy making coffee. As soon as she has done her morning business, she's transformed. She picks up speed and trots back into the house. Time for breakfast.

Breakfast is a big event for Shira – it never gets old. Her eyes glimmer with anticipation as she follows my every movement, skipping back and forth if I get distracted. To her mind, this is my most important task of the day – until lunchtime, at least. When I set her bowl down, she looks at me eagerly and waits for "the word". Then there's no more holding her back, as she plunges her snout into the bowl.

Although Shira eats the same thing almost every day, you'd think I were serving her a four-star menu judging by how excited she gets. She shows enormous gratitude for the fact that her bowl is always full of the same boring food.

I certainly don't mind eating leftovers, but I would probably start to grumble if somebody served me lasagne for the 50th or 100th time. But Shira gobbles up her food every time, showing me the true meaning of daily thankfulness.

It takes so little to show gratitude. Old dogs in particular take real delight in being fed every day, playing in the garden, and sharing cuddles with their owner. They value everything they have, and they make no secret of it.

My Shira is an optimist like me. Is that true of all dogs, or are there pessimists among them too?

A team of researchers at the University of Sydney, led by behavioural researcher Melissa Starling, carried out a simple test to determine whether dogs were optimists or pessimists.[46] First of all, they taught the dogs to associate high and low sounds with particular outcomes: when the high sound was played the dogs were given milk, which they adored. At the low sound they were given plain old water. Before long the dogs were getting excited as soon as they heard the high sound, in anticipation of the delicious milk. When they heard the low sound they were visibly uninterested.

Then the researchers played the dogs a sound pitched exactly between the two notes for milk and water, and observed their reactions. Some clearly interpreted this indeterminate note as a good sign, and their behaviour indicated they were expecting milk. But others associated the sound with boring old water – they were thinking more pessimistically. This led the scientists to conclude that dogs can be either pessimists or optimists, though they found the latter were in a slight majority.

Further experiments by Starling and her team also showed that optimistic and pessimistic dogs behave similarly to their owners. Pessimistic animals expect negative outcomes and don't like taking risks. They aren't depressive as such, but if they suffer a disappointment they get downhearted very quickly. Optimistic dogs, meanwhile, don't resign themselves so quickly if something goes wrong, and are generally less risk-averse.

Another discovery was that pessimistic dogs' cautious approach makes them particularly well suited to working as guide dogs, while optimists are good search dogs, because they are risk-takers and aren't so easily discouraged by failure.

For optimists like Shira, the glass is never half empty – it's always full to the brim. She doesn't grumble through life. While human beings are seldom spontaneously happy, Shira's love of life is inexhaustible. She is happier at the prospect of a walk in the woods than some people are about the birth of their own children.

Being grateful is a choice. Irrespective of our present circumstances, we can choose to be thankful every day for all the good things we have been given, and to push our bad experiences to one side. Of course, gratitude comes most easily when things are going smoothly – but it is precisely in dark times when we need it the most, because gratitude gives us strength, optimism and hope.

Gratitude is one of the fundamentals in life, and I try to make a conscious habit of it. I look for the simple joys that I can be grateful for. As often as possible, I make a note of the little moments of happiness that daily life throws up, and I try to see the positives in everything.

DIARY ENTRY

It's been snowing. And it's cold. -15°C. When I was in Montana for my wolf research it was much colder (-30°). One reason to be grateful for the "warm" weather.

My train to the lecture was 40 minutes late. Typical. When it's cold (or hot), lots of inter-city trains have problems or break down completely – but my train did arrive eventually. And I had time for a cappuccino. Lucky me.

The lecture in Nuremberg was wonderful. The audience was lovely. I'm in a great mood and full of energy. Can't sleep. Tomorrow morning I'll be knackered. But I'm so happy about how well the lecture went. Thank you!

A friend of mine has got herself a positivity calendar. Every evening she writes in what made her happy that day. The phrases she uses most often are things like "red sunset" or "cranes out in the fields" or "blue tits in the trees" – she can always think of something.

I have lots to be thankful for, starting with the fact that I'm alive, I have a roof over my head, and I'm not short of food. I love what I do, and I love my wonderful dog. Every day she reminds me to concentrate on the good things in life, rather than the bad. My optimism may seem naive, but it does me good.

Gratitude is not a one-way street – it also works in reverse. It feels good not just to show gratitude, but also to receive it. Shira's there for me on that front too. Now that she's old, she needs more help from me. I have to give her a boost as she clambers up her ramp into the car, and I help her jump up onto the sofa. She accepts it gratefully. No grumpy "It's fine, I can manage," just a "Whoops! Thanks for the leg up."

I find it difficult to accept help, as I am extremely independent and self-reliant by nature. For me, accepting help – or worse, asking for it – is a sign of weakness. But people who can accept help live happier lives, as proved in a health survey carried out by the German Association of Pharmaceutical Manufacturers.[47] People who find it easy to accept help – from neighbours, for instance – consider themselves happier and more fortunate than people who have issues with it.

Shira shows me there's no shame in asking for help. If she wants me to give her a leg up onto the sofa, she expresses this with dignity and grace: she goes over to the sofa, lays her head on the cushions, and lets her eyes do the talking. "Please may you give me a hand?" And I feel happy and grateful for the opportunity to come to her aid.

18

Where You Belong

—————

Where do you belong? Fewer and fewer people can answer this question. In a world without borders, where nowhere is out of reach, it often feels like there's no room for home in our lives.

Old dogs give us a home, a place of calm, constancy and stability. They know where they belong. Their basket, the toy box, the tin of biscuits in the kitchen – everything has its place. They could find it all with their eyes shut.

Our holiday in Denmark was lovely, but tiring too. The car journey there and back was long, with overnight stops each way, and our daily routine was less fixed while we were there.

On the way back home I noticed how tired I was, and realised that Shira was too. As I laboured through the post and emails that had piled up during our time away, Shira slept for even longer than usual. She looked like she needed a break from the holidays. Although I always take her usual things and her food with us, her mealtimes inevitably become less consistent when we're on holiday. Old dogs find it harder to handle changes in their fixed routine. As I get older, I find the same. I used to be on the road all the time. Constantly moving around and changing my routine didn't bother me, but as I got older, I found I needed a little more time to recover from jetlag following transatlantic flights. These days I'd rather not leave home at all.

I think Shira finds it even more important than I do to have people around her. She feels herself when she's around me. Does she think it's cool to visit new places? I don't know. There are lots of new sights and smells to excite and invigorate her. But perhaps she prefers just going out for the day and then coming back to her own basket for the night. Everyone knows you sleep best in your own bed. When I'm away on book tours, she enjoys staying with my parents, but she misses me and I miss her. And when I come back, she refuses to leave my side, following me everywhere I go. Only then is her world complete again. I am her home and her safe haven.

Cats are said to be more attached to individual places than dogs are. You can't (or at least you shouldn't) take a cat on holiday, but you can take a dog. Shira loves going away with me, but she loves coming home even more.

Home has nothing to do with individual locations. What matters is that you feel a sense of arrival. A sense of belonging. A return to people, animals, nature. A feeling of deep contentment. Happiness. You feel at ease and can be yourself entirely. Home is where the heart is. Home is where the people we love are. Or better still: home is where the dog is.

What did Shira make of our trip? Did I ask too much of her? The journey from Hesse to Denmark was knackering for me, my old dog, and my little 10-year-old Hyundai. To my friends' amusement, I always plan an overnight stop for journeys over 500km in length. I do it for Shira's sake: a few hours in the car at a time, a nice hotel on the way, a lie-in, good food, a nice walk. We travel at Shira speed. As ever, the journey is its own reward.

It's not for me to judge whether a stopover is a good idea, or whether an old dog would rather just do a six-to-eight-hour car journey in one go, sleeping comfortably in the back. But either way, I'd still need some kind of a break – especially as I don't particularly like driving. And a well-rested and even-tempered owner can only be good for an old dog.

That said, I probably won't take my old girl on any more long car journeys in her final years, but will take the train instead, or just stick to places closer to home. Some of my favourite holiday destinations are well within striking distance. There's a little hotel in the Sauerland that I love, only one and a half hours away, in a secluded location surrounded by grassy meadows, with views of the Rothaar mountains, excellent cuisine, and tip-top dog-friendly service. And it only takes two and a half hours to get to the Eifel National Park, where a friend of mine has a small cottage – what I like to call a "luxury break for the elderly".

This summer I'm trying something new: an "adventure holiday" of sorts. I want to know if I can break out of my daily routine without going away at all.

By the middle of the summer holidays, it's refreshingly quiet in my hometown. I've just submitted the manuscript for my new book to the publisher, and have decided to reward myself with a week's holiday. The impending climate catastrophe is the perfect excuse for choosing an eco-friendly holiday destination: Shira and I are going to stay at home and be tourists for a week.

It's a bold experiment on my part, as I don't know if I'll manage to avoid sneaking off to the computer in my study. I unplug it just in case, so I won't get tempted to check my emails, and disconnect the telephone. I'm not available. And no, I don't have a smartphone – that's one distraction I really don't need. I want this to feel like a real holiday.

On the first day of my staycation I have a lie-in, though in my world a "lie-in" means 6.30 am at the latest. As a staunch early bird, I'm usually bright and chirpy by 5 am. I take Shira for a quick leg-stretch while the coffee's brewing, then have my first cup of the day. I'll go without breakfast for the moment and get something to eat in town instead. By the time we reach a cafe at the end of a 40-minute walk, Shira is tired again. She falls asleep under the table on her blanket while I enjoy another coffee and a bread roll on the terrace. We walk back home along the river, and my water-loving old girl refreshes herself with a quick dip.

After such a busy morning, both of us need a rest before we do anything else. At noon, the neighbours invite me over for tea. Jargo, their nine-year-old setter, is infected by Shira's tiredness. The two of them lie back to back on the grass in the sun.

Later in the afternoon, I look through the stack of books I need to read and review. Is that really a holiday activity, or too much like work? Next to it there's a pile of books I just want to read for pleasure. I pick out the one that looks most enticing, and open it. It's an indescribably lovely feeling to be at home, free of responsibilities – a bit like bunking off school.

I take Shira for a final stroll in the deep orange sunset, and then we cuddle up on the sofa as the evening light fades.

Over the following days, I am gloriously lazy. At first I still find it hard not to think about my emails, which are probably piling up by now, but it gets easier and easier to push them out of my mind.

One morning I help Shira up into the car and drive her to the Aartalsee, a small nearby reservoir not far from a hotel where I occasionally give seminars. The reservoir is a paradise for sailors and nature lovers, and the path around it is a popular route for walkers, rollerbladers and cyclists. There aren't many people out and about just yet. When I find a clear spot, I throw Shira's dummy into the water and send her out to retrieve it. If dogs could shout for joy, then the whole reservoir would hear an ecstatic "Woohoooo!" as Shira leaps into the water to fetch it.

After a few dips in and out I dry her off, and we cross the dam to the southern section of the reservoir. She has to stay on the lead here so as not to disturb the birds, since several species that live here, such as whinchats, build their nests on the ground. They are easily disturbed by a nosy labrador. There are 21 artificial islands of varying sizes and surface formations, which have transformed the area into a unique nature reserve populated by many rare bird species. I am glad I brought my telescope, which served me so well in Yellowstone.

A wisp of cloud is floating above the water. We settle down at the waterside and I unpack our breakfast from my rucksack. Shira gobbles up her dog biscuit while I sit with a cup of coffee watching the birds. Using the nature guide *The*

Birds of Central Europe,[48] I manage to identify a good number of them. I see Egyptian geese, buzzards, great crested grebes, coots, goosanders, mute swans, egrets, and a red kite. A hen harrier is on the hunt for mice, and cormorants are drying their feathers on one of the islands. I look for little grebes, tiny divers that are often confused with ducklings, and that can apparently be found in these parts. They like to hide among the reeds in the shallows and are very hard to see. I'm out of luck, and the search tires me out. Shira is already asleep in the grass beside me, so I stretch out on a wooden bench for a while too.

The sun is high in the sky by the time we get up again. At the hotel nearby, I settle down to a salad and a cappuccino on the terrace, and write in my diary while Shira sleeps at my feet. I feel deeply happy.

The holiday gradually draws to a close over the final two days of the week. We go for lots of little walks in the woods and the fields, we visit other friends with old dogs, so that the seniors can have a bit of stress-free playtime, and we spend lots of time cuddling. At regular intervals, I sit down with a book on Shira's warm blanket on the grass with her curled up by my side, fast asleep.

Reflecting on our short staycation, I come to the conclusion that it is perfectly possible to have a relaxed and affordable holiday with an old dog without going away. I have thoroughly enjoyed our time off. No more long car journeys – and I am proud to say that I didn't once turn on my computer. It was the best rest I could ask for. I read lots of books and discovered lots of new walking routes and cafes on our day trips, as well as getting the chance to explore the sights of my own hometown. Shira seems to have enjoyed having me all to herself in familiar surroundings, with no time constraints. If you have an old dog it's a particularly good idea to have a holiday at home – to find out once and for all where you belong.

"So how was it, little one?" I ask Shira on our last evening of holiday, as she lies on her side in the grass, radiating deep contentment, her golden fur shining in the rays of the setting sun.

"We should stay on holiday, if you ask me!"

19

Show
Compassion

Sabine had just heard that her brother had died when her golden retriever Oscar brightly skipped back in from the garden. The moment he saw her he stopped abruptly in his tracks, gazed at her, and then went up to her.

"He laid his head on my knee and looked at me. Then he went away and came back with his favourite squishy toy, which he placed in my lap. He gently licked my hand. I knew he was trying to comfort me," Sabine recalls, swallowing. "I think he instantly felt my pain and hoped that his toy, which always made him happy, would help me too."

How do dogs know what we're feeling? Is it possible that they feel compassion for us? Any show of sympathy requires you to be able to read other people's emotions first. If you have an old dog, your mutual understanding goes way back – so it's no wonder they can sense when something's up.

On a bad day, nothing cheers me up quite like the sight of Shira when I come through the front door. For her, the world is a happy place again the moment I'm back and she can be with me. Empathy requires us to put ourselves in someone else's shoes. For years we thought that humans were the only living creatures capable of this. We denied animals' ability to empathise. It was widely accepted that animals' behaviour was only predicated on eating, breeding and survival. Now, however, scientists acknowledge that we share this highly important, supposedly unique character-istic with several other species. When dogs gaze up at us, they really do penetrate our hearts – it's not an illusion, or wishful thinking on our part. We know when our dogs share our feelings.

Empathy is complex, and its roots are ancient. Over thousands of years, dogs have instinctively learned to please people, often by mirroring the behaviour of their owners. If a person is happy, their dog acts happy, secretly hoping to be rewarded for it. If the person is angry, their dog puts its tail between its legs, feigning sadness as a means of protecting itself from punishment (the reason for which it probably wouldn't understand anyway). If the person is crying, their best friend licks their hand – wanting to be stroked in return.

In order to distinguish feigned sympathy from real empathy, psychology professors Deborah Custance and Jennifer Mayer from Goldsmiths University carried out an experiment.[49] They taught dog owners a noise that sounded more animal than human – something between humming, whining and growling. They then placed the dogs either in front of their owner or in front of a stranger, who either pretended to cry or made the humming noise. Each dog simply acknowledged the humming noise or ignored it entirely, but all of them reacted to crying with care and concern. The use of the humming noise was designed to prove that the dogs' reaction to crying was not one of pure curiosity, but derived from genuine empathy: the dogs clearly ascribed great emotional significance to crying. Furthermore, the dogs consistently responded to the person crying, regardless of whether it was their owner or a stranger. They did, however, care more intensely for their owners – a further sign of genuine empathy.

We all know that *look* that melts our hearts. According to a study at Azabu University in Japan, there is an evolutionary explanation for it.[50] In dogs, as in humans, eye contact releases the hormone oxytocin, which serves an important function in interpersonal relationships – when parents and children look at each other, for instance. In other words, the longer I look Shira in the eye, the happier I am. Could any dog owner doubt that?

It is interesting, though sad, that we humans have more sympathy with dogs than we do with many of our fellow species. Researchers came to this conclusion following a study on empathy, in which they examined the reactions of people to a fictitious crime.[51] When small children and puppies were presented as the victims of the crime, they received the most sympathy. Next in line were grown-up dogs, with adult humans in last place. The reasoning for this is simple: we instinctively have more sympathy for the weak, defenceless, and innocent. A dog needs protection in our eyes, much like a small child or a puppy does, while we consider grown-up human beings robust enough to defend themselves.

Do our dogs feel empathy for other animals as well?

The behavioural scientist Marc Bekoff tells a story about his dog Jethro, who he adopted from an animal shelter.[52]

"I knew he was a very special dog. He never chased the rabbits, squirrels, chipmunks, or deer who regularly visited. He often tried to approach them as if they were friends.

One day Jethro came to my front door, stared into my eyes, belched, and dropped a small, furry, saliva-covered ball out of his mouth. I wondered what in the world he'd brought back and discovered the wet ball of fur was a very young bunny.

Jethro continued to make direct eye contact with me as if he were saying, 'Do something.' I picked up the bunny, placed her in a box, gave her water and celery, and figured she wouldn't survive the night, despite our efforts to keep her alive.

I was wrong. Jethro remained by her side and refused walks and meals until I pulled him away so he could heed nature's call. When I eventually released the bunny, Jethro followed her trail and continued to do so for months."

We all want to protect our pets. The older they get, the more we want to shelter them from the ugly sides to our world – and that includes insensitive remarks about our dogs. Non-dog-owners might not be aware of the tactlessness of some of the things they say, but they can be very hurtful.

My friend Laura has a 12-year-old alsatian who is visibly ageing. He's gone grey, he's not as slim as he used to be, and he walks with a heavy limp. But he is still full of love and zest for life.

Who would be so cruel to go up to someone and say, "Is that your mother? Wow, she looks awful. She can hardly move! She can't have much time left." But owners of old dogs frequently have to put up with that kind of nonsense from complete strangers. I was asked Shira's age on one of our walks, and was met with the response, "Have you thought about putting her to sleep? She's pretty old now, isn't she?"

I'd have liked to reply, "You're a pretty slow walker too. Do you ever wonder how long you've got left?" But I didn't say it, because I'm a decent human being and don't take pleasure in putting other people's noses out of joint.

The Wisdom of Old Dogs

Clearly some people assume they can say anything they like about a stranger's dog. If you have an old dog, every single day you already have to face up to the fact that it will probably die soon. But there's a difference between me thinking about it and being clumsily reminded of it by someone I've never met.

The final years and months we spend with our furry friends are the most bittersweet time of any dog-lover's life. We know from the moment we get a pet that our hearts will one day be broken. But the older our best friends get, the more loveable they become, and it is only once they have reached the absolute peak of their magnificence, and we simply can't love them any more than we already do, that they die.

So I beg you: if you walk past someone who is standing around, waiting patiently for a grey-muzzled old pooch plodding along slowly behind them, show some compassion and think before you speak. Say something nice about the old boy, ask them whether you can stroke him (not all old dogs like being touched), and show him the affection he has earned just by virtue of being older and wiser than you. No more than that is required, but certainly no less.

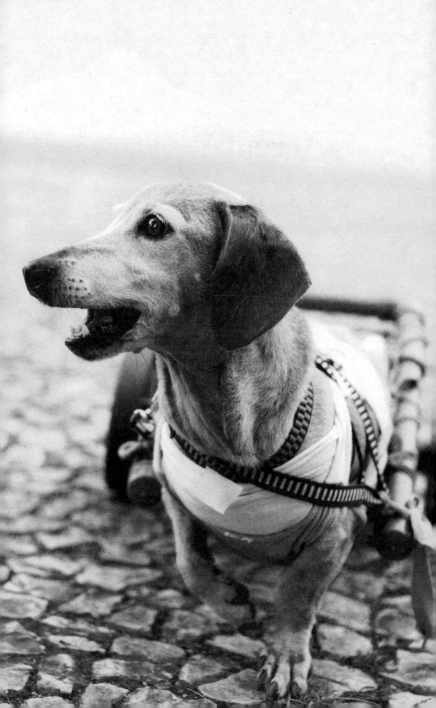

Accept What
You Can't Change

As I flicked through the newspaper at breakfast this morning, I lost my appetite. Trumpism, extremism, racial violence – a world in chaos. Beside myself, I threw the paper down onto the table. "What on earth is wrong with humanity?" I called over at Shira, who was lying on her blanket, waiting patiently for her biscuit as I tore my hair out.

At that moment I wanted nothing more than to go back to my log cabin in the wilderness. While I lived there, I went without electricity, internet or TV. The battery radio only broadcast regional gossip, weather forecasts, and country music from the local station – there were no earth-shattering news reports to speak of. It was heavenly. I had rarely been so relaxed. If a war had suddenly broken out, I wouldn't have known a thing about it. I longed to return to that world of peace and quiet.

But here I was in Germany, wired up to the internet, with more news reports flooding in than I knew what to do with. It had got so bad that I had begun to suffer from stomach aches, high blood pressure, and insomnia. Getting worked up about things wasn't doing me any good – especially as my outrage at the world didn't make a jot of difference. What's more, it all cost me valuable energy, which I needed now more than ever. I was already stressed as it was – I had a seminar looming over me and needed to finish preparing for it.

I looked over at Shira lying sphinx-like on her blanket, her head resting on a teddy bear, watching me with a look on her face that held all the wisdom in the world. How I envied her! A deep sense of calm radiated from every fibre of her light labrador fur.

"How do you do it?" I asked her.

Perplexed, she looked up at me with inquiring eyes. "Huh?"

I knelt down next to her and took her head in my hands.

"You live a happy life, and you don't take any notice when the world's falling apart all around you. Don't you ever worry about anything? Getting old? Dying?"

I felt her head move as her tail began to wag.

"Been there, done that," she replied.

"Ooh, smarty pants."

"Hey. I'm old. I've seen it all before. My joints might be hurting today, but I know they'll be better tomorrow. Life goes on."

"And that's it? The big secret to staying calm and composed?"

She snorted her assent and laid her head back down on her teddy bear.

But I was still curious. "And if your dog food ran out tomorrow and there were no more treats? What would you do then?"

Shira's head jerked to attention and she looked at me incredulously.

"Okay, okay, only joking," I laughed reassuringly.

Shira gave my face a lick. Her world was whole again.

Been there, done that. Seen it all before. The poise of an old dog is enviable – and extremely desirable.

"God, grant me the serenity to accept the things I cannot change, courage to change the things I can, and the wisdom to know the difference."

The famous Serenity Prayer is attributed to several different sources and appears in a number of variations, one of them courtesy of Friedrich Schiller: "Blessed is he who has learned to bear what he cannot change, and to give up with dignity what he cannot save."[53] Nowadays, it is best known as the closing prayer of anonymous self-help groups such as Alcoholics Anonymous.

The Serenity Prayer gave me a very particular idea for Lent this year: I decided to give up outrage.

In the weeks leading up to Easter each year, it is traditional for Christians all over the world to prepare themselves for the feast by giving something up for Lent, which begins on Ash Wednesday and ends on Holy Saturday. Millions of people give something up every year in order to get themselves out of a rut. The idea is not just to renounce chocolate or nicotine, but to use the fasting period as an opportunity to re-evaluate: seven weeks of scrutinising your daily routine, adopting a new perspective, and discovering the things that matter in life.

I decided to give up outrage after reading about the author and blogger Johannes Korten, who took his own life in the summer of 2016. In his suicide note, the highly sensitive and empathetic author wrote that he had been shattered by modern life, particularly by the threats of global terrorism and mass shootings. I find it tragic and unconscionably sad that it is the compassionate people with so much to give who are broken by this world.

This spring, I had reached a point where I was in desperate need of a calmer outlook on life. So "seven weeks without getting outraged" became my own private motto. I did keep watching TV and reading the papers, but I simply acknowledged the news, took a step back in my mind, took a deep breath, and let go.

And, astonishingly, it worked. By the end of Lent, I was palpably more relaxed. I had realised that I couldn't prevent chaos in the world, and that it was no use getting worked up about it. Why should the words and deeds of others affect my own feelings and wellbeing? Nobody apart from me is responsible for how I feel.

Giving up outrage did me so much good that I continued to incorporate it into my daily life and general attitude beyond Easter. If my friends remark in amazement how much more relaxed I seem than before, I smile enigmatically at Shira as she lies in her basket, snoring loudly. It's her who taught me to keep it together.

Our dogs don't need the Serenity Prayer. They're the absolute masters of serenity and acceptance. Old, ill and dying dogs accept their fate. They don't complain about how unfair the world is, nor do they ask, "Why me?" They just play the hand they are dealt.

Alex is a veterinary physiotherapist. She gives my Shira regular treatment to strengthen her muscles and keep her limbs moving. Another patient of Alex's is Buster, a 10-year-old male crossbreed, who was partially paralysed in a car accident.

"His owners wanted to put him to sleep, because they thought his quality of life would be next to zero," Alex tells me. "But I could see how much sheer joy he still took in life." She fixed him up with a "wheelchair" adapted for dogs – really more of a cart than a chair, with a frame made of lightweight metal, and harnesses at the front and back that can be adjusted with snap buttons to fit the dog. It is nimble and handy off-road, thanks to its air tyres. Now he's got used to it, Buster can scoot around with his doggy pals as if he still had all four legs. He has a fun life and delights in every new day with his humans. Even dogs who have lost limbs to cancer, or who have been crippled by age and arthritis, can be instilled with new zest for life. Martina's eight-year-old dachshund had a slipped disc and invertebral disc disease. On his wheelchair, he is now so nippy that his owner has fixed little BMW hubcaps to his wheels.

"It's unbelievable," says Alex, with tears in her eyes, "how astonishingly well animals come to terms with an illness or handicap, if we just give them a chance. If you give them lemons, they make lemonade."

There are times in all of our lives when things don't go to plan. But there is always a solution. Composure means being able to stay calm, collected, and detached in difficult situations. It is the opposite of restlessness, agitation, anxiety, and stress.

Recently I was stuck in traffic. The whole motorway was at a standstill. The driver in front of me took the fact that he couldn't move forward as a sort of personal affront, ranting and raving at the wheel. The woman in the vehicle beside me was nodding along to music, and the whole car was rocking with her. She was singing at the top of her voice and was evidently happy in herself and in the world. Both drivers were in the same situation, but they interpreted their positions totally differently. For the man, the traffic meant anger and frustration, but the woman was completely relaxed. Both had the power to make whatever they wanted of the situation they were in. It was their choice to get worked up about it or not.

Life isn't fair. We have to accept that as a fact and bear it with stoicism – an attitude that will spare us disappointment. Our future lives come with no guarantees. If you're on top of the world, a fall might be coming your way – or it might not. Anything can change at any time. We can lose everything we have in one instant. So we should be happy with what we have – even if it's just a bone – and make the most of it. But we must remember that anything can be taken away from us at any time, including our lives.

Philosophers as far back as Socrates, Aristotle, and Seneca have repeatedly asserted that real happiness is inseparable from cheerfulness and composure. Accept what you can't change: this pearl of wisdom has stayed with me over the decades and has significantly simplified my life. How often do we do our own heads in, trying to alter the unalterable? How many people can truly say they've never got angry about something they couldn't change? What do we get out of it, apart from headaches and upset stomachs?

My mother invented her own serenity motto at the ripe old age of 87. "I don't get worked up any more. It spoils my beauty," she tells me with a mischievous smile.

Every day we encounter situations where we can practise staying calm. And every day, old dogs show us how it's done.

Mabel, my friend Corina's nine-and-a-half-year-old Bordeaux mastiff, is a prime example. Mabel is one of the happiest and most optimistic dogs I've ever known. She greets every new day with a broad grin on her crinkled face. Anyone who sees her rampaging around the garden, ears drawn back and chops flapping about, with her best friend Emma the rottweiler, would never imagine what this dog and her owner have had to endure together.

At the age of three, Mabel had to have surgery on her elbow, and there were five more operations to come over the course of her life. She even had to have gold bead implants inserted into all her joints during one of the procedures. Every time she looked to have recovered from her latest operation, she suffered another setback shortly afterwards. The worst thing was that Mabel's kidneys eventually couldn't handle all the narcotics, painkillers and antibiotics anymore. Every operation meant fresh worry for Corina. She would sit with Mabel for hours, holding the drip bottle, trying to feed her with her hand. Mabel's heart and kidneys were severely damaged, and several times it was touch and go. On one occasion, Corina only managed to save her dog with a heart massage. Corina's friends advised her to let Mabel go, questioning whether it was really worth putting herself and her dog through all of that.

But giving up was out of the question. So my friend kept fighting for her beloved dog, through weeks of fear, hope, and doubt. Each time Mabel's condition got worse, Corina was on red alert, listening to her every breath. When Corina heard the news that her sister had died, she held her sick dog in her arms as she wept. Sometimes the cruel hand of fate seems too much to bear.

Eventually Mabel's condition began to improve, and things seemed to be taking a turn for the better. Life granted the pair a few years brimming with joy and hope. But Corina's fears remained.

"When I see Mabel playing with Emma, I hold my breath," she says. "But I can't wrap her up in cotton wool. She's such a cheerful, fun-loving dog, and she relishes every good moment she gets."

Mabel's illness is a significant emotional and financial burden on my friend. But still she struggles on, even when all hope seems lost. Corina knows that she will have to let Mabel go in the foreseeable future. That, too, will be an act of love.

"We have an agreement. Mabel has promised me to make it to 10 years old no matter what. Then we'll at least have one more summer… Back in 2012, nobody apart from me and my vet thought she'd even manage another four years. She's a medical miracle, still full of life and spirit – sometimes you'd think she was only nine months old. She makes me laugh, but she also makes me cry all the time. She's my one and only, my joy, my soulmate. We've experienced so much together, and we've always pulled through. She's been with me for a decade of my life, and I just hope she'll stick to our deal."

"When you look back on your life together, knowing everything you know now, would you take on all of that again?" I ask Corina. I already know the answer – it's the same answer I'd give.

"Of course! The good moments far outweigh the bad, and I've learned to live with my fears and worries, to take them as read and not rail against things, but enjoy every minute I have with Mabel and be there for her – as long as I possibly can. It's been well worth the fight. And when Mabel leaves me one day, I will have made peace with the inevitable. I've done everything I can to give her a great life."

We live in a quick-fix society with technology that can repair almost anything, but we forget that everything in our lives has to come to an end one day – including us. When that happens, there will be nothing more to repair. Optimism and fighting spirit are all well and good, but at a certain point optimism becomes nothing more than denial. It is important to struggle on as long as it is advisable to. But one day we will reach the point when it's time to stop, when we must stop seeing death as the enemy. That doesn't mean giving up, but simply accepting what happens to everyone.

Four weeks after my conversation with my friend, Corina had to let Mabel go. Her body had given up. Mabel couldn't keep her promise any longer.

Accept What You Can't Change

Mabel's extraordinarily gracious acceptance of her situation, no matter how bad it was, demonstrates one of the most valuable traits of dogs – old dogs in particular. They don't shy away from things, and they don't fall into depression. They never stop taking pleasure in life and making the most of it. Nothing changes in their behaviour, their bright and cheerful optimism. No matter how bad their situation is, they accept it. That is a lesson we can all learn from.

A crucial element of a life of calmness and composure is trust. We cannot avoid sorrows, illnesses and catastrophes, but we will survive them. If we believe in ourselves and practise living in the moment, we can put things right again.

I have decided that from now on I will relish the adventure every new day brings. I will accept every situation life throws at me, no matter how desperate it seems, and I will turn it inside out and see what I can make of it. The most hopeless of situations are actually key moments in our personal development, because they force us to make peace with what is happening, regardless of the outcome. Old dogs teach us one of the most precious lessons of all: now is the moment to seize life by the scruff of the neck. Don't worry about what things might look like tomorrow. Each new day will bring its own delights and difficulties, but today's worries are quite enough for now. Everything else will happen in its own time.

Overcome
Your Fears

In March 2018, after a warm start to spring, there was a cold snap. Overnight temperatures dropped to -10°C and there were 20 centimetres of snow. Shira, who loves the snow, was lolloping around in the garden, and wandered onto the sheet of ice covering my little garden pond. Had she forgotten what was underneath?

I was just putting my snow shovel away in the shed when I saw Shira stepping onto the pond out of the corner of my eye.

"Shira! No!"

In the same instant, I heard the ice crack and saw her forelegs slowly sliding into the dark water, which had opened up beneath her, before her whole body plunged in. Frantically, she tried to pull herself back up onto the ice, but it kept breaking under her weight. She splashed about in a panic, then saw me running over and paddled towards me. My pond is small, but it has an artificial basin with vertical walls, so she couldn't climb out by herself. As Shira wasn't wearing a collar, I couldn't pull her out by that either.

Finally I made it to the pond and jumped straight into the water in my winter clothes. The water came up to my waist. Shira clambered onto me and I lifted her up onto the bank, before climbing out myself.

It wasn't a dangerous situation for me, but it was for Shira. I had only just finished clearing the snow at the front of the house, so if she had fallen through before I came back round, she could have drowned or frozen to death within a minute. When I saw my dog in the water, I didn't pause for a moment to consider if and how I could get her out. I acted on pure instinct.

Only later, back in the house, as Shira was drying out in blankets and towels by the radiator and I was warming myself up with a cup of tea, did fear begin to creep into my limbs. I sat down next to my old girl.

"Did you have to choose today of all days as the start of the swimming season?" I asked her. I took her head in my hands and inhaled the smell of her damp fur. "We got lucky there, didn't we?" Relief enveloped me like a warm coat.

Shira looked deep into my eyes, snuffled heavily, and went back to sleep. To her I was probably a hero. Her knight in shining armour. Wonder woman. After a while, that was actually how I felt – though my legs were still shaking.

People love heroes. We write books and make films about them. We give them awards and accolades. But what actually makes a hero? There are as many answers to this question as there are people to ask. For some, it's police officers, firefighters or paramedics – people who save lives. For others, it's whistleblowers or journalists who stand up for freedom of speech in totalitarian states. Some of our heroes suffered a violent death, such as Dietrich Bonhoeffer, Mahatma Gandhi and Martin Luther King, while others are living among us: single mothers and fathers, teachers, pastors, and politicians who take a stand against hate and violence.

They all show mental and moral courage every day of their lives. And by courage I don't mean not being afraid, but taking action *despite* being afraid.

My first dog, Klops, was once attacked by an alsatian who had been terrorising the whole neighbourhood with his aggressive behaviour. As the dog sank his teeth into Klops's neck, Klops shrieked in excruciating pain and desperation, but the alsatian wouldn't let go. I dashed in, threw myself on Klops's assailant, and prised his jaws open with both hands to set Klops free. I sat on the raving alsatian, pinning him to the ground as my dog lay whimpering beside me. Only then did I realise I had a problem. I couldn't let go of the alsatian's snout, because he might bite again, and he might go for me next. So I stayed where I was, acting as a human muzzle for what seemed like an eternity before the alsatian's owner finally came running and hauled him away. Did I think about the fact the alsatian might bite me before I acted? No, it didn't cross my mind in the moment. The adrenaline coursing through my veins forced me to react, no matter how bad an idea it might have turned out to be.

Was I brave? It wasn't courage that saved my dog from his attacker. It was pure instinct – a mother who saw her baby in danger. I would strangle a sabre-toothed tiger with my bare hands to keep Shira out of harm's way.

When I told a non-dog-owning friend about it at the time, she was gobsmacked. "Would you also jump into a fast-flowing river to save your dog?"

"Yes, I wouldn't give it a second thought."

"What about a stranger's dog?"

"Absolutely."

"What if it meant putting your own life in danger?" My friend couldn't get her head round it.

"I still would. I'd be grateful if a stranger helped my dog. Wouldn't you do the same to save your child? Or someone else's child?"

"Of course." And then came the remark you so often hear from people who don't have pets. "But that's different."

A dog in danger often brings out the best in us – but just think how often dogs risk their lives for their owners!

My friend Mike, his dobermann King and his labrador Boomer were an inseparable team. One evening Mike was cycling through a quiet side street with his dogs on the lead, when a van came around the corner and knocked him off his bike. He fell head first onto the tarmac, and the driver fled the scene. Mike's first instinct was to look round for his dogs. Boomer was standing on the pavement and King was in the middle of the road. Mike staggered towards King, calling out to him, but King ignored him, looking in the other direction. "I assumed he was dazed after the accident," says Mike. "I certainly was." He was still about 10 metres away from King when another car turned into the street. Horrified, Mike tried to reach his dog as quickly as he could, shouting, "King! King!" King turned and looked at him, then turned back and began to walk straight towards the onrushing car.

"He knew I was injured – I didn't know it myself, I was thinking more about him. He stayed in the middle of the road just to protect me. And then the car hit him. My God, I'll never forget that moment."

Boomer reached King before Mike did. He grabbed his friend by the collar, trying to pull him out of the road.

"I couldn't see how badly King was injured, but I knew it was serious, because he wasn't moving."

The second driver bolted too, leaving Mike standing there covered in blood in the middle of the street. A local resident fetched a blanket, which they used to wrap King up in while they waited for the veterinary ambulance. They took the dog to a veterinary hospital. He was in a critical condition, and had suffered a traumatic brain injury.

"I had to put him to sleep – it nearly killed me," says Mike. "He was my first dog, and he's still with me, here in my heart."

After a while, he got a new dobermann as a pal for Boomer. "Life goes on. But not without a dog."

Nothing demonstrates the strength of the bond between us and our dogs better than the silent burst of empathy that prompts us to act when a dog is in danger. We forget all reason, because reasoning is so much slower than simply knowing what to do. We act on gut feeling, as our instinct to protect takes over. That instinct is reserved for our nearest and dearest – whether they walk on two legs or four.

Dogs don't just save people, they protect each other too. On YouTube you can find a number of heartbreaking videos of dogs trying to save their injured friends, or even sacrificing themselves for them.

One video particularly moves me.[54] A badly injured female dog has collapsed on a railway track bed in Ukraine, and a furry friend comes and lies down on top of her to protect her. Then the film shows an onrushing train that goes straight over the pair of them.

Fortunately, the track bed was deep enough that the dogs didn't come to any harm. They stayed there for two days in the freezing cold, until their fur became coated in a layer of ice. It proved difficult to get the pair off the tracks because the male was so determined to protect his friend, but eventually the rescue operation was successful. On examination, they discovered that the female was badly bruised, but otherwise healthy. The owner was found and took the dogs back home.

Another video shows an injured dog on the motorway. The dog lies motionless in the middle of a lane, with cars racing by. Then another dog runs into the road, grabs his chum by the collar and tries to drag him to the hard shoulder. Nobody slows down for them, and one car even appears to strike them a glancing blow on its way past. But the dog carries on undeterred and eventually drags his companion to safety.

There are endless stories of courageous dogs saving lives! We used to doubt whether animals were capable of selfless behaviour. It was thought that dogs only acted in the interests of their own survival. These days we know better. Even wolves behave altruistically.[55] During my research in Yellowstone, I once witnessed a turf war where a wolf was attacked by an enemy pack. His friend broke up the attack by running close by the fight, diverting the enemy wolves' attention towards himself. Both of them survived.

In another fight I witnessed, a courageous wolf was less fortunate. He jumped right into the fray, "sacrificing" himself for his family. He was killed.

Among the earliest evidence of selflessness that we have can be found in the ruins of Pompeii. Situated in the Bay of Naples in Italy, Pompeii lies in the shadow of Mount Vesuvius, the most famous volcano in the world. At around 10 o'clock in the morning on 24th August 79 AD, tremors shook the region, buildings caved in, and then there was an earth-shattering boom as Vesuvius erupted and a gigantic black cloud burst out of the crater. Ash began to rain from the sky as lava and mud flowed down into the valley, destroying Herculaneum, the neighbouring town, in its entirety.

Most of the inhabitants of Pompeii were killed by lethal phosphorous gases, and were buried under a layer of ash several metres thick. Once the ash cooled and solidified, the corpses rotted away, leaving behind hollow spaces that archaeologists later cast in plaster, thus preserving the forms of the buried humans and animals for all to see.

One plaster cast particularly moves visitors to the site: a mould of a little dog lying on top of a child. The dog, named Delta, is wearing an engraved collar that states he had already saved the life of his owner (or perhaps his owner's son), Severinus, three times.[56] On one occasion he pulled the boy out of the sea, saving him from drowning; on another occasion he fought off four robbers who attacked Severinus; the third time, Delta protected the boy from a fierce wolf. His final act of heroism was to throw himself over the child to protect him from the deadly ash cloud.

Dogs are heroes – but unlike police officers or firefighters, they have neither financial incentives nor health insurance. They will save a baby from a rushing river and get a bone as reward. It's no big deal for them. Heroism is standard for dogs. They don't act bravely just to prove their mettle. They are genuinely selfless, and that is an example we can all follow.

People can suppress their fears out of love for their dogs, even in the most tragic of circumstances. This is demonstrated in a stirring story about a dog and its owner living in the Warsaw ghetto during the Second World War. The Jewish writer Isaiah Spiegel spent part of the war in a Polish concentration camp that the Nazis built in 1940. He wrote the story *A Ghetto Dog* for a post-war anthology.[57]

Spiegel depicts the brutalities of ghetto life from the point of view of an old, frail, lonely widow and her equally frail old dog Nicki. The Germans have begun to shoot all the dogs in the Warsaw ghetto on the grounds that they are "Jewish" dogs, and the widow can't bear the thought of leaving her companion to face his fate alone. She follows him out of the ghetto to the pen where the dogs are to be executed. She takes Nicki's lead with her, wound tightly around her arm like the tefillin[58] scrolls used in orthodox Jewish rituals, and dies together with Nicki.

To me, this story about an old woman's love for a dog in the cruellest of circumstances is a testament to true heroism.

Courage is often silent. Courage is standing strong and holding out when you want to run away. Courage can also mean simply listening instead of talking, or telling the truth when you'd rather change the subject. It is an act of courage to express your feelings when you're sad, scared or hurt.

A vital component of my relationship with Shira is my vow to protect her. I keep this promise as faithfully as I can, even if it means going out of my comfort zone or getting into dangerous situations. Or just getting cold and wet.

I have found that my desire to protect my dog gets stronger and stronger the older she gets and the older I get. I am afraid something might happen to Shira. A bigger dog might hurt her at play. Her limbs are creaky nowadays and she's not as agile as she used to be; playfully jumping up on her could break her back. She could be run over by a car she fails to hear because of her deafness. A dog she's never met before, whose growled warnings she doesn't hear, could take her for an intruder and attack her. Yes, I worry about her. And that worry never goes away.

How do I deal with it? I have to recognise that some things are out of my control. Like Corina, I can't wrap Shira up in cotton wool. I have to let myself be afraid. Fear is part of life. I can be scared of something and still do it – that's what makes life such an adventure. Fear is not a barrier; it is a cloud that we can walk right through if we so choose. By facing up to my fears and putting on a brave face, I can learn how to handle different situations in life and gain greater self-awareness, like when I oppose a well-known dog trainer's objectionable methods, or when I stand up for my dog's defects in the face of criticism. And the same applies when I take Shira in my arms – undeterred by the scorn and superiority of other dog owners – when she's scared during a thunderstorm. These are the little tests of courage that we have to face each day with an old dog, and that make us their heroes.

But I will need more courage than ever at the end of our time together, when I will have to face my worst nightmare and let go of the love of my life. In that moment, I will be making good on the promise that I made her when I first took her into my care: I will always love you, and will lead you safe through the darkest times.

There's a Time
for Everything

Over the course of our lives, there are many things we have to leave behind. We let go of our physical and intellectual abilities, our unrealistic expectations of ourselves and others, partners and children who leave us to go their own way, and dreams we can no longer fulfil. For instance, I've always dreamed of going to space to see the world from above. Space tourism is supposed to be the market of the future, but the fact is that due to my age and lack of spare change (the seven space tourists who have visited the International Space Station since 2001 paid around 20 million dollars each), I won't be able to live this dream within my lifetime. I'll save it for the next one.

Saying goodbye is part of life. Letting go is hard to start with, but it gets easier and easier. We let go of the most important things in our lives last of all.

When we first get a dog, we know that we will lose it one day. We don't want to believe it, because it's still a long way in the future − a whole lifetime away. We can't and won't even consider the possibility that it could be tomorrow. We keep death at arm's length, but the distance becomes shorter and shorter the older we and our dogs get. Only when time is running out do we really begin to take every day as a gift.

Sigmund Freud once said, "At bottom, nobody believes in their own death."[59] And it's true, although of course we all know we have to die one day. Nobody escapes death. But we still try everything we can to outsmart it, or to convince ourselves it won't happen to us. We make desperate attempts to keep age and death at bay, through sport, healthy eating, skin creams, plastic surgery... And we're outraged when people who've smoked and eaten badly all their lives end up living longer than others who've done everything "right". Life simply isn't fair.

Sometimes, when I'm sitting in my armchair engrossed in a book, I find myself keeping an ear out for Shira's snoring. If the familiar noise stops, I'm suddenly on full alert. Is she still alive? She raises her head, as if my sudden fright has woken her up, and looks at me sleepily. "Everything okay?"

"Sorry. I'm just scared of losing you," I tell her, knowing full well that I am going to lose her. "Not yet. Sometime in the future," I add.

"I'm still here." Shira lays her head back down on her forepaws and starts snoring again.

How can I put my love for my dog into words? Can I quantify it by how afraid I am of her death? How can I bring myself to let go without forbidding her to do anything that could bring her to harm? For her and me to live happy and fulfilled lives, I must simply let her live – despite all the risks that life brings.

What if I knew the date of her death – or mine – in advance? Could I live carefree and enjoy every moment till then? Or would more and more last-minute panic set in with every passing day? Would everything that life is about pass me by as I waited for that day to come?

The greater our love for our dogs, the more difficult we find it to cope with their impending death.

And yet that is exactly what we must do. Only when we are ready to look death in the eye can we learn to live and love with openness and clarity. If we shrink from death, we shrink from life.

Does Shira actually know she will die? If so, how would she want it to happen? In my living will, I have outlined in detail how I want to die. But what do our dogs want? They can't tell us. Do they really want to die in our arms, or is this yet another instance of us imposing our own preconceived ideas on them?

It has been claimed that people can consciously choose their moment to die. A friend of mine nursed her father through the final weeks of his life, caring for him round the clock, never leaving his side. He died at the precise moment when she had gone into the next room to talk to the doctor, leaving him alone for a few minutes. "Why, oh why?" She had wanted to be there – to be there for him. But when someone is dying, it doesn't matter what *we* want; all that matters is what the dying person wants.

We can't know whether clinging tearfully onto our dogs as they get the lethal injection is an imposition that they only accept out of love, or whether they would perhaps rather die alone in their favourite spot in the garden, like Max.

Max was my friend Annelie's 11-year-old hovawart (the one who got to choose "his" new car). He had been ill for a long time. His owner knew he didn't have long left, and did her best to make everything as pleasant as possible for him. During the nights, she had to let Max out into the garden more frequently than before. On his last night, he wanted to go out once more. "He went outside and rolled around joyfully in the grass, as he often used to," Annelie recalls. "When I called him in, he just lay there as if he'd fallen asleep. I went over to wake him up. Then I saw that he was dead." Together with two friends, Annelie carried Max into the house, and they all sat down around him to bid him one final farewell. A death like this – as painful as it may be – is what we would all want for our dogs, and perhaps for ourselves too.

Many wild animals also withdraw from company to die. Old wolves don't say goodbye to their families; they simply get up and walk off – sometimes to their favourite places – to die alone.

Very few people are properly aware of the finiteness of their lives. When we are young, the very idea of death is non-existent – still a good 70 or 80 years away. If we lose someone we love, death abruptly draws nearer. But our dogs are the ones who really make us aware of the fleetingness of life. Their lives are so short! As death approaches them sooner or later, we finally acknowledge the prospect of our own death too, and start searching for answers to life's fundamental questions:

What really matters to me? What have I messed up? Is there anything I wish I could do again? How did I see the world when I was young? What will be left of me? What would it be like if I knew how long I still have to live? What am I waiting for? How much time do I have left?

Entering old age with an old dog reconnects us with the fundamentals of existence. Do dogs ask themselves about the meaning of life? I want to know what it is, so I crouch down next to Shira, who looks up at me expectantly.

"Walkies?" her eyes ask.

"Nope. Philosophy session."

She breathes out heavily with a mixture of irritation and disappointment. "Fine, get on with it."

"Do you ever ask yourself whether your life mattered, and what mark you made on the world?"

Shira raises and lowers her eyebrows alternately. She always does that when she's thinking.

"Here's the thing," I continue. "Lots of people seem to have crises at some point in their lives. They up sticks to go and live in the forest, or buy themselves a motorbike, or get a younger girlfriend. For them, life seems to have been emptied of excitement and new challenges. They realise they've just been sitting back and letting life run its well-trodden path. We're talking about people who have everything they could possibly need – and yet they're still unhappy."

"Well, I'm happy."

"Really? You're 13. Have you never had a crisis? What's the meaning of life for you?"

Out it comes like rapid fire: "Eating, sleeping, swimming. And tennis balls."

I feel a little twinge that I haven't made the list.

Is there a greater meaning to life? Or does life carry its own meaning? Does the meaning of life simply consist of living your life as it comes, like Shira does?

Dying is as individual a process as living. Death means change: we say our goodbyes and let go. But we have to live before we can die. It is precisely the finiteness of our life on earth, the knowledge that we can't hold on to a moment for ever, but must relish it, because we can never get it back, that should make us treasure every single day. This transience is what makes life so precious. We can't prevent death, but we can be prepared for it.

In 1990, when I got my labrador Lady from the animal shelter in America, my world was overflowing with happiness, joy, and hope. But deep inside me, of course, I knew that one day – in 10 or 15 years – she would break my heart. Lady's 15-year countdown came to an end at Easter 2005.

It was a dazzlingly beautiful morning, the clear blue skies speckled with a few cotton-wool clouds. But far off on the horizon, dark clouds were gathering. I listened to Lady snoring and snuffling beside me. She was asleep – finally. She had been wandering restlessly around the house the whole night long, until eventually I gave her a sedative and an anti-sickness tablet. For a few months she had been taking medication to help her heart and her hydration levels, and I had recently started giving her the maximum dose of Metacam to ease the pain and inflammation caused by her arthritis. I was grateful for a few hours of quiet – for her sake as well as mine. There hadn't been many nights lately that I had slept through uninterrupted, and I was truly exhausted by this point. Even now, part of me was on red alert, listening out for every sound she made. Soon Lady would wake up again and carry on wandering around the house, limbs trembling because her muscles were so weak, ears drooping and tail between her legs because she found it all so tiring. She would start to pant again, gazing at me with her big brown eyes. Then I would take her in my arms and try to calm her. She would wriggle away and ask to be let out into the garden. But there, too, she would just wander around for hours, driven by inner restlessness and pain. I would administer her next dose of tablets and hope they worked. My heart bled for her during these periods of unrest. I wanted to help her so much, but there was nothing I could do.

The German cabaret artist Jochen Busse once spoke candidly at an event about his retirement, saying, "At 72, death isn't yet at the door, but he's out there looking for a parking space."[60] In Lady's case, death was just parking up – and I couldn't stop him approaching our front door.

I still wasn't ready to let go of the most precious thing I had, even though I'd had plenty of time to prepare myself. I hadn't wanted to believe it, but my dog's age could only mean one thing. For a big pedigree dog, 15 is a good innings – though there are always exceptions. Some dogs make it to 16, 17, or even 18 years old, like my neighbours' dog (who lived his whole life tied up in the cellar or in the garden). Life just isn't fair.

My heart had known much longer than my head that it was time. For no apparent reason, I had been thinking about death for a long while. I had been reading Elisabeth Kübler-Ross's wonderful books on dying, and had been preoccupied with the idea of death on my most recent trip to Yellowstone. My neighbours in my log cabin were hunters, and when I walked out of my front door in the morning I was often shocked at the sight of dead elk loaded onto the back of their pick-up truck. I saw animals die in the park – not killed quickly and naturally by predators, but suffering alone, in agony. I saw a bison mother and her calf who had fallen through ice into the lake beneath. The pair couldn't get out on their own. I had to bear witness to the slow, lonely death of the two animals. The mother drowned first, which kept the calf alive for a little longer as it climbed up on its dead mother to stand on her. But it couldn't stay out of the water for long. I spoke to the park rangers and begged them to save the creature – but they showed no understanding, remarking that things like that just happened in nature.

At the time, it didn't cross my mind that it would soon be my turn to "deliver" an animal... And I had only just got back home when I heard that two friends had died and my best friend had been diagnosed with cancer. I was literally surrounded by death.

Death is a subject I am constantly grappling with, because I think we can learn a great deal from it. Thinking about it has helped me grow and mature. I have considered it in detail, made sense of it, and come to terms with it intellectually and spiritually. I even welcomed it when my first dog died, and when I was able to be at my grandfather's side when he died. These were very special, wondrous, painful moments – moments that changed me and my life for good.

Letting go is an act of love. It rests upon the profound recognition that life runs its own course and doesn't cling on beyond that. Animals understand this fundamental law of nature. It is only us humans that are always fighting against it.

All my life I have liked having everything under control. But the situation with Lady forced me to face the fact that it was all out of my hands now. Everything I had learned on my journey so far meant nothing anymore. I had to accept the situation, in order to make dying easier for Lady. I had to keep the faith and let go of my need to micromanage every moment. Giving up does not mean accepting defeat – it has nothing to do with winning and losing. It simply means giving something back to the universe that we didn't and couldn't create on our own.

I had prepared myself for Lady's death. When she began to go markedly downhill in her final weeks, I started reading countless books and talking to friends who had also lost dogs. The vet and I discussed how to proceed when the inevitable happened, and she gave Lady a final blood test, which showed that her kidneys were beginning to shut down. The numbers were considerably higher than normal, and she had all the symptoms of kidney disease. She was drinking vast amounts of water, and her urine was very bright: that meant her body was no longer flushing out toxins properly. She had lost control of her bowels over the previous few months, though I could live with that. More recently she had started suffering from balance problems, another symptom of kidney failure, as well as nausea.

Now that I understood the time had come to let Lady go, all my preparation went out of the window in an instant and I was taken over by raw, agonising pain. I clung to one last glimmer of hope: when she was asleep, breathing peacefully, I prayed that her agitation had just been short-term and that she would recover after all. Or I hoped that in her deep slumber, she would slip gently over the rainbow bridge into the world beyond. But it wasn't to be. Just as I had taken responsibility for her almost 15 years ago when I adopted her from the animal shelter, fate now required me to take one final step: it was time for me to relinquish her and help her on her way home. I wrangled with God, begging Him for more time: "just until the summer", "a few more days", and eventually, "just one more night".

Lady, loving creature that she was, would certainly have been prepared to give me a few more days, even if they had been a struggle for her. But I couldn't possibly have forced her into that. When I rescued her from the animal shelter, I promised I would always be there for her. Now the time had come for me to deliver on that promise.

By Easter Monday, Lady had reached a point where the bad days outnumbered the good. I could no longer think about my own life: all that mattered was my dying dog. I wanted to approach the end of her life with the same dignity and stoicism that she was displaying. Only when I was ready to let her go would she be able to depart this world unafraid. Once I realised that, my fear gave way to acceptance.

Lady slept through the days, exhausted, and at night she wandered about. Her heart problems seemed to have led to anxiety episodes; she wanted to be close to me all the time. I took her in my arms and comforted her. I gave her the pills that had helped her up until now, but they barely seemed to work anymore. I was utterly drained and numb. I lay down to sleep next to my dog – on the sofa, sometimes even on the floor – and stroked her. If she fell asleep for a little while, I crept back to my own bed. A short time later she'd be standing in front of me, panting, looking at me, asking for help, her tail between her legs, the corners of her mouth drawn back. I could see she was in a bad way. She was suffering. That afternoon she had still been able to play with me, jumping around for a little while before heading out for a walk. I was well aware that the hours immediately before death are often marked by a deceptive return of energy. Lady briefly seemed to recover her strength – but that was merely a sign of her impending departure. Back in the house, she began to stumble more and more, no longer able to co-ordinate her legs.

The next morning, Lady fell into a deep, peaceful sleep. Again, I asked myself whether we might yet be able to wait a little while. But my dog put my doubts to bed when her breathing problems returned.

I took her head in my hands and looked deep into her eyes, which shimmered with a strange, deep lustre. Her tail beat heavily on the floor. She looked at me peacefully, almost tenderly, for a long moment. No words were needed. We had said everything there was to say.

I reached for the telephone and called the vet. "It's time," I said. She still had patients to see, and agreed to come over after she'd finished. We had two hours left. By this point, love was far more important than my fear of loneliness.

This is the final gift our dogs give us: the gift of letting go. It is not a gift that we want, or that we are prepared for. We must leave it to our dogs to lead us out into the unknown, fortified once more by their love and loyalty.

Let Go of What You Can't Hold On To

That phone call with the vet began the hardest but most beautiful time I had ever spent with my dog. I was grateful that I could stay by her side at this crucial moment in her life. This worst of days was to bring me wonderful gifts. People whose relatives have died suddenly often regret that they didn't get the chance to say goodbye. They wish they had been able to say all the lovely things we rarely get round to in our day-to-day lives. But now I had the opportunity to say all the important things to Lady once more. I lay down on the floor next to her, stroked her, and spoke to her.

"It's okay to die," I began. "You know I'm going to miss you terribly. I wish you could stay with me forever, but that isn't possible. I know the place you're going to now is beautiful, and we'll never really be apart. If you have to go now, I'll help you on your way." I swallowed the lump in my throat, ignored the burning pain in my heart, and continued.

"You know how sad I'll be when you're no longer with me. But my memories of the years we spent together will stay with me forever. Don't you worry about me, things will get better in time."

I asked her advice one last time. "Are you sure you're ready?"

Her warm gaze told me all I needed to know. "Time to let go."

The decision was made. I felt calm once more – relieved, even. We were embarking on this final journey together, with love in our hearts.

I gave her all the treats she had always liked so much. She probably thought she was already in heaven. I kissed her muzzle, her head, her paws, and told her she was about to go on a long journey to a beautiful place where there was water to swim in and plenty to eat, and where many of her old friends were already waiting for her. I told her she would see her mother and siblings again. I crossed my heart that she had nothing to be afraid of, and I promised that I would come to find her one day, and then we would never part again. Once more I told her how much I loved her, and I asked her forgiveness for letting her suffer for so long and for doing what I was about to do. We looked into one another's eyes, talking without speaking.

I held her in my arms until the doorbell rang. Lady, who was almost deaf, somehow heard the bell and shot to the door, barking enthusiastically – suddenly the young dog she had once been. Taken aback, the vet looked at me searchingly. "Are you sure?" I described the last few nights to her. She knew I wouldn't be making this decision if it wasn't in my dog's best interests.

Lady lay down peacefully on her blanket under the window. The sun gave her fur a radiant golden glow. She had never been as beautiful as she was at that moment. I gave her one more biscuit while the vet prepared the anaesthetic. Holding Lady's head in my lap, I thanked her for everything she had given me, and said a silent prayer. "Thank you, God, for this dog you gave me, to bring unconditional love and happiness into my life. She did a truly wonderful job. The time has come for me to give her back to you. Take care of her."

The vet injected the anaesthetic into a vein in Lady's hind leg. The muscles convulsed momentarily and then relaxed again. Her body went soft, sinking deeper into my lap. I caressed her head. She was still breathing, but had sunk into a deep sleep. My last words to Lady were, "Walk into the light. Safe journey. I love you."

Then the vet administered the lethal injection directly into her heart. Its effects seemed no different from the anaesthetic, apart from the fact that Lady's pupils went milky. She was no longer breathing. My dog was dead. I wished I had a second heart that I could slip into the place of this broken one.

The vet asked if there was anything else she could do for me, and when I said no, she gave me a hug and left the house without another word. I was alone with my dog. I held her in my arms and stroked and stroked her. I felt her warmth and the softness of her fur. It was as if she were asleep – only she wasn't breathing anymore. Then there was a twitch in her legs. The vet had warned me: "It can happen that her muscles go into spasm, although she's dead. That happens because commands from the brain are still effectively being carried out."

I took in every moment, every millisecond, as deliberately as I could. I knew that Lady was dead, but the twitching made me feel there were still remnants of life left in her. I was like a little girl covering her eyes with her hands, hoping that when she took her hands away everything would be back to how it was before. But nothing was the same anymore. I looked out of the window. Two buzzards flew across the blue sky. Lady must be flying away up there somewhere – free of fear and pain.

According to *The Tibetan Book of Living and Dying*,[61] the dead stay with us for a little while after they have shuffled off their mortal coil. The death of the brain is not the end of the dying process: the length of time between the last breath and the end of "inspiration" is traditionally described as "the time required for eating a meal", so around 20 minutes. During this time, the deceased are still spiritually present, even if they are already physically dead. This, and the period immediately following it, is for many people the most intense experience they have ever shared with their pet.

After a while, I gently laid Lady's head on the floor, went into the garden, picked a few flowers, and arranged them around her. I photographed her lifeless body. I cut a few hairs from her, which I would later bury in some of our favourite places as a token of remembrance. Then I made myself a cup of tea and got out my old photo albums. Cup of tea in hand, I sat back down next to my dead dog on the floor and rested her head in my lap. As I stroked her, I looked through the many pictures I had taken of her. I told her about the time I rescued her from the animal shelter in Virginia, and how we had been destined to find each other. I told her about the trips we had undertaken together. Choking back tears, I couldn't help laughing about our adventures. "Do you remember when we went to Arizona and clambered up the red rocks in Sedona, and lay down on the warm sandstone at the top? I wanted to experience a vortex, one of those whirls of energy that the place is known for. We fell asleep there and only woke up when a coyote started howling next to us. You were so frightened you nearly jumped out of your skin – and the coyote did too."

I enveloped us in memories with my stories of times past. I asked her, "Did I do the best job I could have done? Were you a happy dog?"

I was overwhelmed by lovely memories and deep gratitude for our time together. I knew she had had a good life. Yes, she had been a happy dog – I was sure of that.

One by one, my parents, neighbours and friends came over to say goodbye to Lady. I still couldn't let her go. But that was okay. Eventually dusk fell. Lady became increasingly cold and stiff. Slowly, slowly I began to let go of her in my heart, as her body changed in minute, imperceptible ways.

Only now, nearly eight hours after her death, did she really seem to have gone. Suddenly I knew that her soul was no longer in her body. What was left in front of me was only her outer shell.

Finally, I was ready to bury her. I wrapped her up in her favourite blanket, laid her to rest in the grave I had dug for her in the garden, and tucked one of my worn t-shirts underneath her head, so my smell would remain with her. Around her I placed her lead, her favourite toy, a photo of her and me and – in accordance with ancient Egyptian tradition – a few treats for the long journey; after all, labradors are always hungry. One last kiss, one last stroke. Then, with a little prayer, I tipped the first shovel-load of dark, warm earth down onto my dog. It was over.

By the time I had filled the grave, I was drained and utterly exhausted. But I did feel that her end had been a dignified and peaceful one, and I knew I'd done things the right way.

That night, Lady brought me a parting gift. I heard the clicking of her claws on the floor, and a short while later I heard her shake herself. Although I couldn't see her, I could smell her and could feel her presence distinctly. Her spirit was sending me signs that she was well. She didn't want me to be sad.

Many dog owners are not granted the opportunity to say such an intense goodbye to their furry friends. In many cases, circumstances don't allow it, or they are simply not in a fit state to accompany their pets on their final journey. My first dog Klops was put to sleep at the vet's surgery, and circumstances beyond my control meant I had to leave him there. Because of that, it took me much longer to heal after his death. Being able to stand by our four-legged companions in their final weeks and days is a special blessing and a rare gift that we should gratefully accept. It is a fulfilling and profound experience. And as painful as this process is, we grow from it.

Death used to be part of our lives. When my great-grandmother died, she was laid out in her living room for three days. Her daughters prepared her, washed her, dressed her, and laid her out in the casket. We all got the chance to say goodbye to her, and the neighbours came round with some food for us all. We stood or sat around the dead woman, talking about the times we spent with her. When things calmed down and everybody had gone again, I crept back into the room alone and talked to my great-grandmother. I felt as if she were still there. I found this opportunity to say goodbye very curative.

These days we have forgotten how important such rituals are. People die quietly, behind closed doors. Preparation of the body is left to the undertaker. But we still can't just let go. If people are missing and presumed dead, we spare no effort to find them and bring their body home. When thousands of people were killed in the World Trade Centre on 11 September 2001, specialist teams went out with search dogs to look for the slightest remains, for the sole purpose of giving certainty to the families of missing people. Only that could offer them some kind of closure.

Spending so much time with my dead dog enabled me to find peace. When I held Lady in my arms after her death, I discovered a feeling of pure gratitude, deep love and bright light shining through the pain. This feeling is the same every time – whether the deceased is a beloved animal or a person. Perhaps the moments after death grant us a glimpse into paradise…

So why is it that we're so scared of death? Nobody can say what it's like to die, unless you count near-death experiences. I imagine death as a homecoming. Perhaps it is much nicer on the other side than we imagine. We simply don't know. But fearing death while you're still alive is senseless. Animals, and old dogs in particular, teach us to live every moment of our lives consciously, right up to the very last. To lead a fulfilled life, we must forget our fears.

Our dogs show us how to accept suffering without complaining, and how to get the best out of life in the face of age and illness. And when their final hours are approaching, they acknowledge their impending end calmly and deliberately. Lady accepted death with a poise that I hope I will one day be brave enough to emulate.

Cry, Laugh, Love

A dog's life is short, too short. But you know that when you enter into it. You know that grief awaits you one day – you will lose your dog and suffer because of it. And that is why you should relish every last moment and share in your dog's joy every single day. The idea that a dog can be your companion for the rest of your human life is an illusion – nothing more and nothing less. But there is a peculiar beauty in this brutal truth, and in the fact that we give our dogs our hearts in the full knowledge that the price we will pay for it is utterly unconscionable. Perhaps our love for our dogs is a form of atonement for the illusions we create for ourselves, and for the mistakes we make as a result of these illusions.

There is little room for death and sadness in modern society. But for those of us who live with an old dog, the anticipation of grief permeates our whole lives. Our relationships with dogs are dictated by a mountain of feelings – from simple sadness and melancholy to the most intense feeling of happiness we will ever experience. It hurts to witness the deterioration of an animal that you love, but at the same time, this period of change is more precious than any other. The closer our relationship was, the deeper our sadness. That is the price we have to pay for love.

I once heard a story about the Buddha and a woman whose son had died. She went to the Buddha and asked him to help her overcome her grief. "My son is dead," she told him. "Please bring him back to life."

The Buddha promised he would. The woman's grief began to abate at the very thought of having her son back again soon.

"But there is something you must do first," said the Buddha. "Bring me three stones. Each one must come from a person or family that has never suffered a loss."

The woman set off on her search for three people who fulfilled these conditions and could give her a stone. It was a long time before she went back to the Buddha. She came empty-handed.

"I didn't find anybody who could give me a stone," she said.

"And what did you learn from it?" the Buddha asked.

"I learned that all of us suffer, and all of us lose someone or something we love."

The death of a dog is a terrible occurrence for which we can expect little comfort from others. Grief for an animal still frequently goes unrecognised. When we lose a person who is close to us, then we are allowed to grieve openly – for a certain period of time. When we lose a dog, we must bear it all in complete silence, as if nothing has happened.

But people who skirt around grief often struggle to exhibit real joy or spontaneous happiness either. Our feelings are all bound up in one another. People who do not connect with their negative emotions are unlikely to feel positive ones so intensely either. Light and darkness belong together – they are equally important parts of a bigger picture.

Grieving for a beloved creature is a sacred time in our lives – and an important one too. The Swiss doctor Elisabeth Kübler-Ross is a pioneer in thanatology, the study of death. In the 1960s, she began to research the psychology of human beings following a bereavement, and concluded that there are predictable phases that people go through when they are grieving.

It starts with a shock to the senses. Our perception of the world is suddenly dampened. When Anna lost her husband at the age of 62 after a long illness, she was in shock, but she came to terms with her loss astonishingly well. Lulu, her little poodle, was a great help and comfort to her. Over the course of the next three years, Lulu increasingly took on the role of her deceased husband, becoming her one and only. But then Lulu died. This time, Anna was overwhelmed by grief, and was rushed to hospital with massive heart problems. Her intense grief for her dog was met with little understanding from her family, so Anna put on a brave face – but behind closed doors she transformed her home into a shrine to Lulu, with pictures and toys everywhere and her ashes on the mantelpiece. Only later, during psychotherapy sessions, did she succeed in probing the deeper reasons for this. Anna had never undergone a proper grieving process following the deaths of her husband or her dog. Moreover, she felt extremely guilty that Lulu's death had hit her harder than that of her husband. The therapy sessions also brought to light that Anna had suffered a miscarriage when she was younger, and hadn't properly mourned her lost child either. So she had already suffered two bereavements that had deeply affected her before the loss of her dog finally let all her pent-up emotions loose. It was a long time before Anna, with the help of her therapist, was able to process all her suppressed feelings. She now has two cats.

Grief is nothing unnatural – it is a completely normal reaction to an overwhelming loss, even if it's "just" a dog. Over the course of our lives, our dogs become part of us. When they die, that chapter in our lives is over. We will probably lose more dogs than partners or children during our lives, so we have to go through the stages of grief much more often with them. Each time we have to confront grief and come to terms with it, we become older and wiser, and discover more memories to look back on. Painful experiences are fundamental for our personal development.

Loss does not mean losing something, feeling sad about it, and then going back to the old status quo. We will quite possibly never be the same again. But that's exactly why grief isn't a waste of time. It has much more to do with the self than with the sadness we see and feel. Life transforms us – beneath, during, and as a result of suffering. The experiences we least want to go through are often the ones that change us the most. But we can trust that things will turn out for the best. When grief is tearing us apart, life takes us in its hands, and love moulds us like wax into new shapes. We must suffer the pain of loss because if we never experienced it, we'd be incapable of sympathy with other people, and we'd turn into entitled, egocentric monsters. The dreadful pain of loss teaches our proud species humility, softening even the most callous of hearts. We are never as strong and full of love as we are when we're at our most vulnerable.

After this initial shock, one of the next predictable stages of grief, according to Dr Kübler-Ross, is disbelief and denial. We cannot accept that our dog is not around anymore. This is an example of the human mind's self-defence mechanisms at work. Mild hallucinations are not unusual during this stage of grief. I heard Lady's footsteps, smelt her damp fur – a smell I particularly loved – and heard her shake herself. Reason is the last thing to enter our thoughts and feelings at this stage. We would give anything just to put an end to the intense pain we are suffering. So we turn to prayer. Why not? If God sees how seriously we mean it, couldn't he just work a little miracle for us? Miracles do happen – we know that much. All over the world, the impossible is made possible. Why shouldn't the same happen for us when we are grieving? We jump at the tiniest glimmers of hope, losing ourselves in fantasy. This is particularly common if the dog owner didn't actually witness their dog's death – if the creature suddenly vanished, for instance. We are always hearing stories of animals turning up again after years. Why shouldn't our dog do the same?

Marga, whose dog Paul disappeared one day and didn't come back, tried bargaining – which is the next stage of grief. "I held out the crazy hope that by some miracle he was alive and well somewhere. So I prayed, 'Please, God, if Paul comes home safe, I promise I'll take better care of him than before, I'll take him for more walks…'"

At some point we give up hope and give in to intense pain and total despair. This is the moment when reality sets in. We give vent to all our suppressed feelings of anger and guilt, and we take it out on everyone. On ourselves: what did I do wrong?

On the vets: why couldn't they save my dog? On God: why did my dog have to die, a creature overflowing with love in a world full of murderers? And even on the dead dog: why did he have to run into the road when he should have been walking to heel? Or: why has he abandoned me? He could have fought on a little longer!

We swipe out at everything, even at people who have our best interests at heart. A well-meant but insensitive phrase like "Get another dog, then" enrages us. Our friends don't mean any harm – they are just helpless in the face of an intense grief they don't understand.

But the anger we feel is a sure sign of our deep love for the animal we have lost, and it shows us we are making progress, because we can now admit feelings that we previously shut out. Anger often goes hand in hand with feelings of guilt – a normal reaction to duties that we neglected.

When we take responsibility for an animal, we are promising to be there for them and to take care of them at all times. Death plays no part in our plans. When it comes, we are taken over by a sense of complete failure. In our hearts and minds, we agonise over what might have been if only we'd done things differently. We took on a godlike role in our dog's life, and we couldn't fulfil it. No matter how much love we poured out, we could not change the way of the world.

Sally was an old stone-deaf retriever, the darling of her family. She was enjoying the twilight of her life on a homely farm, spending most of her time sleeping in the sun. One day she was accidentally run over by her owner Carl, the farmer, in a tractor. She lay down in a blind spot behind the wheels, not hearing that the engine was still running. Carl was inconsolable. "If only I'd just got out and checked one more time."

Christa's dog Sandy always walked off the lead, even in big cities, but stayed obediently by her side. Christa was convinced "she obeys me". One day a cat ran out into the street right in front of Sandy, and the dog's perfect obedience went out of the window for the briefest moment. She was hit by a car and died. Her owner couldn't stop beating herself up. "If only I'd just kept her on the lead!"

Things happen. We're only human – we're not gods. Some things are beyond our control, and we have to accept that we make mistakes.

Feelings of guilt weigh particularly heavily on us if we have to have an animal put to sleep. Couldn't we have waited a little longer? Or were we too late – did we let the poor creature suffer for too long?

Guilt. It's unavoidable. Often we don't deserve to feel guilty; sometimes we do. But how long should we keep cultivating feelings of guilt? At some point we have to look inwards and begin to love ourselves again. We must forgive ourselves. The painful memory of what has happened will never leave us, but nor will the wonderful experiences and the love we shared with our beloved pets. If our dogs were sitting in judgement of us, they would probably long since have forgiven us.

Elisabeth Kübler-Ross delineates the close relationship between feelings of guilt and time: "Since guilt always comes from the past, it keeps the past alive. Guilt is a way to avoid the reality of the present. It drags the past into the future: a past of guilt will create a future of guilt. Only when you release your guilt do you truly release your past to create a new future."[62]

"Guilt is the gift that keeps on giving," so the saying goes. It seems to last forever. Even when we begin to discover happiness once more, we destroy this positive feeling by believing that we no longer deserve to be happy. We need courage in order to forgive ourselves.

Our dogs loved us despite all our failings. They saw the good in us. Now is the moment we have to look for the good in ourselves once more and rediscover it. Let's carry on being the wonderful people our pets knew us to be.

Following this whirlwind of feelings comes a silent period of depression, during which we cannot imagine ever being happy again. Depression is a real danger for our health. Under severe emotional strain – which can be caused just as easily by the death of a dog as by the loss of a relative – people can literally die of a broken heart. The Japanese call it "takotsubo syndrome", a form of cardiac malfunction that constricts the heart and sends it into spasm. The symptoms resemble those of a heart attack, and can be acute enough to kill.

I have previously witnessed the phenomenon of "heartbreak" in wolves. The alpha male and female in a pack usually stay together their whole lives. When the alpha female of a pack I was observing died, her partner followed suit just a few days later, a matter of metres away from her, without apparent cause. The subsequent examination showed that his heart had packed up.

On the other hand, depression can be a first step back out of grief, as it forces us to face up to reality. The worst is over. For the first time since the death of our furry friend, we can envisage an end to our suffering and see a tiny speck of light at the end of the tunnel.

Lady had been dead for a few weeks. Now and then the pain seemed to be ebbing away, absorbed back into daily life. Then something happened: I went into town to pick up a few things from the shops, and saw a dead squirrel lying in the road. Cars were driving around it – no one seemed to care. I stopped, picked the little creature up, carried it out of the road, and set it down under a tree. Its body was still warm and soft, and a little blood was running from its nose. Presumably it had been hit just moments before. I laid it gently on a bed of leaves, covered it with more leaves, and said a short prayer to send it off to squirrel heaven. As I went back to my car, I couldn't help thinking of my

Lady, who had had a passion for chasing chattering squirrels up trees. I wondered whether that was what she was doing, wherever she was now. On the way home I stopped off at our favourite field, where we had gone for shorter strolls, particularly during the final few years when she was having a bit more trouble walking. I remembered the warmth of her lifeless body and the times when she used to run across this field – already slightly stiff in the legs – snuffling over the grass, on the hunt for new scents. A wave of grief hit me suddenly, like a punch to the stomach. I couldn't hold back the tears, and I felt horribly alone. It was a long time before the pain abated and the good, happy memories prevailed once more.

At some point we become too exhausted to continue grieving, struggling, trying to change things that cannot be changed. We give up and let go. Only then can the healing process begin.

Slowly but surely, I began to look outwards again. The pain was no longer so intense, although I still had mood swings. I managed to sleep through whole nights uninterrupted, and my appetite returned. My body got back into the rhythm of things. It didn't happen overnight. Sometimes I just went out of the front door, only to break down in tears the moment I saw the neighbour's dog. The first time I hummed along to a tune on the radio, after a long period of sadness, I gave myself a fright. Where had that voice come from? Was it right for me to sing again?

Elisabeth Kübler-Ross sees this final stage of grief as a time of inner growth and healing. It is a time when we can let go of the pain we have suffered, without being disloyal to our memories.

We will carry on, and we will love again, but what we have lost will remain in our hearts forever.

It is said that time heals all wounds. This is not entirely true, because some wounds will always hurt and will leave scars. We must learn to live with them, and to turn them into wonderful memories. That is the best way we can honour our deceased pets. As time passes, we will not love them any less, but we will feel less and less overwhelmed by the idea of death. We will learn to let go of pain and to cherish our memories – a process that will change us. Life with dogs spoils and enriches us. When it is over, we must honour them by making the most of what remains of our lives, and by becoming better people.

I would like to share two more sad and heartwarming stories with you. The first is about a dog who couldn't forget his dead owner.

We often hear stories about grieving dogs who would not leave the side of their dead master or furry friend. The most famous of these stories was adapted for a film called *Hachiko*, starring Richard Gere, which brought millions of viewers to tears.

Hachiko, whose original name was Hachi, was born in November 1923 on a farm in the north of Japan. He was a pedigree Akita, an ancient Japanese breed. His owner, Hidesaburo

Ueno, was Professor of Agricultural Science at the University of Tokyo. The childless academic took great care of Hachiko, talking to him, playing with him, and feeding him. Hachiko grew up to be a big, strong Akita, over 60cm tall, more than 40kg in weight, with thick cream-yellow fur, a corkscrew tail and pricked-up ears. Every morning Ueno let Hachiko accompany him to work, usually to the nearby Shibuya train station. His dog would pick him up there again in the evenings – come rain or shine.

On 21 May 1925, Hachiko waited as usual for Ueno to come back. But when the train drew in that evening, the professor didn't appear. In the middle of a lecture, he had had a brain haemorrhage and died.

Undeterred, Hachiko returned to the station to wait for his dead owner at the same time every day – for 10 whole years. He became so famous that there was even a monument built to him, in the form of a big bronze statue. When Hachiko died, thousands of people poured into the station to decorate the place with flowers. A Buddhist monk said a prayer for the dog. Today Hachiko's stuffed body is on display in the National Science Museum in Tokyo. In Japan, he continues to be a symbol of loyalty and solidarity.

The second story is about a child's grief and a stranger's empathy. In October 2006 a letter to the editor was published in the *San Antonio Express-News* in Texas, which later re-appeared in several newspapers. It is a true story.[63]

Joy Scrivener, from San Antonio, wrote:

"Our 14-year-old dog, Abbey, died last month. The day after she died, my four-year-old daughter Meredith was crying and talking about how much she missed Abbey. She asked if we could write a letter to God so that when Abbey got to heaven, God would recognise her.

She dictated and I wrote:

Dear God,

Will you please take special care of our dog, Abbey? She died yesterday and is in heaven. We miss her very much. We are happy that you let us have her as our dog even though she got sick. I hope that you will play with her. She liked to play with balls and swim before she got sick. I am sending some pictures of her so that when you see her in heaven you will know she is our special dog. But I really do miss her.

Love,

Meredith Claire

P.S.: Mommy wrote the words after Mer told them to her

We put that in an envelope with two pictures of Abbey, and addressed it to 'God in Heaven'. We put our return address on it. Then Mer stuck some stamps on the front (because, as she said, it may take lots of stamps to get a letter all the way to heaven) and that afternoon I let her drop it into the letterbox at the post office.

For a few days, she would ask if God had got the letter yet. I told her that I thought He had. Yesterday, for Labour Day, we took the kids to Austin to the Natural History Museum. When we got back, there was a package wrapped in gold paper on our front porch. Curious, I went to look at it. It had a gold star card on the front and said 'To Mer' in an unfamiliar hand.

Meredith took it in and opened it. Inside was a book by Mr Rogers, *When a Pet Dies*. Taped to the inside front cover was the letter we had written to God, in its opened envelope (which was marked 'Return to Sender: Insufficient Address'). On the opposite page, one of the pictures of Abbey was taped under the words 'For Meredith'. We turned to the back cover, and there was the other picture of Abbey, and this handwritten note on pink paper:

Dear Mer,

I know that you will be happy to know that Abbey arrived safe and sound in Heaven! Having the pictures you sent to me was such a big help. I recognized Abbey right away.

You know, Meredith, she isn't sick anymore. Her spirit is here with me – just like she stays in your heart – young and running and playing. Abbey loved being your dog, you know. Since we don't need our bodies in Heaven, I don't have any pockets! So I can't keep your beautiful letter. I am sending it to you with the pictures so that you will have this book to keep and remember Abbey.

One of my angels is taking care of this for me. I hope the little book helps.

Thank you for the beautiful letter. Thank your mother for sending it. What a wonderful mother you have! I picked her especially for you.

I send my blessings every day and remember that I love you very much. By the way, I am in Heaven and wherever there is love.

Love,

God, and the special angel who wrote this after God told her the words."

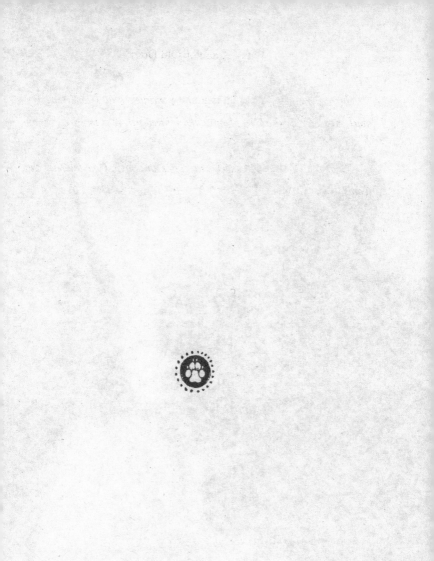

Love
Never Dies

Anyone capable of love knows that love is not thwarted by death. We continue to remember, cherishing each and every memory. We visit graveyards, and we place urns or pictures in special places on our shelves. Sometimes we even build great monuments like the Taj Mahal in India, a mausoleum that a Mughal emperor had built in memory of the deceased love of his life.

In October 2001 I flew to the USA to interview an artist who had constructed a unique monument to his dead dog.

It was a cold winter's day in Vermont. The trees had cast off their leaves in a majesty of colour. I drove through the small town of St Johnsbury, searching for its most famous attraction.

At the end of a secluded cul-de-sac, a little white New England church appeared on the hillside, its tower reaching up into the clear blue skies. The weathervane at the top of the tower was not the traditional angel, but a black labrador with wings. In front of the church there was a carved white wooden sign with four labradors and the message, "Welcome all creeds, all breeds. No dogmas allowed." Those were the only rules that applied here.

Next to the chapel, in a large white farmhouse in the classic New England style, was a gallery. Here I had arranged to interview one of the most unconventional artists in America, Stephen Huneck.

On entering the building I had to step over a well-fed labrador, who stuck out his tummy for a long stroke. In the studio I was met by Gwen, Huneck's wife, who showed me a collection of the most imaginative and wacky pieces of art I had ever seen: wooden chairs with jumping fish for backs, a coffee table held up by four carved labradors, a table lamp with a stand made out of a dachshund standing on its hind legs, and a bench formed of two wooden dalmatians. The American lifestyle magazine *Home & Garden* had recently labelled these works "the striking, successful madnesses of Stephen Huneck".

A loud vroom announced the artist's arrival as he groaned up the mountain in his enormous Hummer, making deep furrows in the unsurfaced road. He parked up, and a golden retriever – visibly slimmer than the labrador – leapt out of the car. The stocky, dark-haired man greeted me heartily and invited me for a tour in his four-wheel drive. After a short but bumpy ride over open ground, we reached the summit of Dog Mountain, as he had named it, from where we had a view over the whole area. Here Huneck had built another monument to his dog: a carved winged labrador perched on top of a marble column.

Then he told me his story, and the story of the Dog Chapel.

The oldest of seven children, Huneck wasn't allowed to have a dog when he was younger, although in his heart of hearts he wanted nothing more. "We were poor and couldn't afford a dog," he said. "At 17 I left home to go and be a hippy. That was when I got Shirley, my hippy mongrel."

Shirley became his "business partner". After finishing his art studies, he started going from door to door with her, collecting antiques – or "junk", as it called it with a chuckle. He began renovating old furniture and making unusual wooden sculptures. On a cold winter's day in 1984, he loaded one of his wooden angels into his pick-up, and had just arrived in town when he noticed a man staring at his truck. It turned out he was a well-known art dealer from Madison Avenue in New York. That was Huneck's lucky break. The first work of his new career was a carved wooden dalmatian puppy.

By the mid-90s, Huneck's works were appearing in expensive galleries and even museums all over America. But his fame still hadn't reached the masses – until a fateful accident turned his life upside down.

In 1995, Huneck was carrying a 60kg wooden dog sculpture down a flight of stairs when he fell, breaking several ribs. "In hospital, I contracted a rare and often deadly viral infection that attacked my lungs. I was in a coma for two months; the doctors weren't holding out much hope. My wife refused to believe I wouldn't make it. She didn't leave my side. One night the doctors told her it was touch and go."

In actual fact, Huneck was clinically dead for five minutes, and had a near-death experience during that time. Two weeks later he woke up from the coma, to the doctors' astonishment.

"I had to learn to walk again at the age of 45. We often had service dogs visiting us in rehab, and they had a hugely positive impact on my recovery. It's unbelievable how spiritual dogs can be. They have a strength that few people fully understand."

On his long road to recovery, Huneck began to make wooden carvings of his black labrador Sally and to write books. He illustrated every book with woodblock prints.

"In the months following my recovery, I thought about life and death a lot. I thought about the rituals we perform when someone dies. We throw a handful of earth onto the lowered coffin, to symbolise that the dead person is returning to dust.

This helps the living find closure. Since dogs are also family members, I thought it would be wonderful if we could create a ritual space to ease the pain when we lose a beloved dog, and to bid them a final farewell."

At the foot of Dog Mountain lay the chapel, the gallery, and Stephen Huneck's home. Between them was a little lake, in which a group of dogs was happily splashing about, as visitors looked on with smiles on their faces.

Huneck turned to look at me. "You've got a dog too, haven't you? I can see it in your face."

"My labrador, Lady, is back in Germany. I miss her terribly."

"Then you'll like it here," said Huneck. He kept talking as we went back to the car. "There's one evening at the start of my recovery that I remember very clearly. I was knackered, because my muscles had wasted and I was having trouble moving from one room to the next. Suddenly a thought hit me: build a Dog Chapel. At first I was incredibly excited. Then I thought about how much money my medical treatment had already gobbled up. With what was left, the most I could build was a small kennel."

For months the thought wouldn't leave his head. And eventually, in 2000, he decided to build a chapel with his wife, as a symbol of the spiritual bond the couple had forged with their dog. The church would be open to both dogs and people. He built the chapel on his farm in St Johnsbury, in the style of a little Vermont village church from the 1820s.

I approached the building with reverence. Going through the front door (which had a built-in dog flap), I stepped into a room whose walls were covered several times over with pictures of dogs and handwritten notes, letters and prayers – not unlike a Bavarian pilgrimage chapel. Photos of dogs with birth and death dates, along with notes written by visitors about what they meant to them, showed that this was a place to pray and give thanks in the name of Dog.

"Duke, we miss your sneezing when we stroked your tummy."

Beneath a drawing of a dachshund someone had written, "I miss you, Frank, my little hot dog for 16 years. Thank you for all the happiness you brought me." I felt the visitors' grief and sensed the closeness of the bond between them and their dogs. Suddenly I was overwhelmed with longing for Lady.

On two maps of the world, brightly coloured pins showed which countries visitors to Dog Mountain had come from. Every continent and country was represented, from Saudi Arabia to Tanzania. I added a red pin to Germany.

The central figure in the room was the now familiar wooden labrador angel atop a column. I moved forward into the chapel itself, and was bathed in bright light glittering through the stained-glass windows. They were decorated with pictures of dogs being stroked by human hands, licking ice cream, or looking directly at me with their tongues hanging out. The four rows of pews were flanked by sitting wooden dogs, and there was even a doorknob in the shape of a dog's head, with "All creatures welcome" engraved around it.

Wooden labradors kept guard at the near end of the chapel, sitting on carpets decorated with dachshunds, pugs, and more labradors.

This chapel was the largest and most personal of Stephen Huneck's works. "It's a place where people can celebrate their spiritual bond with their dogs."

The Dog Chapel isn't a real "church" in the traditional sense of the word. "We aren't allowed to hold services here," the artist explained. "But we organise special events on several weekends each year when we bless and celebrate our animals."

Of course, dogs are not only allowed everywhere, but are positively welcomed.

"It's a sad fact that dogs don't live as long as us. I had to have a dog put to sleep who I had shared a roof with for 14 years. It nearly killed me," Huneck said. "I wanted to build a place where people could say goodbye, but where they could also have as much fun with their dogs as possible."

For that reason he laid out footpaths, an obstacle course, and ponds for dogs to swim in. In winter, visitors bring their animals to go hiking in the snow and enjoy the unspoilt countryside.

"Dogs bring us closer to nature, helping us to live in the moment and to feel loved unconditionally. They give us so much and demand so little in return."

Dog owners are grateful to Stephen Huneck. They come here with their dachshunds, great danes, alsatians and poodles, sit in the chapel, whose doors are never locked, stroll around the extensive premises, and visit his gallery. There has not been a single biting incident, according to Gwen. Perhaps the dogs are equally affected by the peace and quiet of the place.

Stephen Huneck hit cult status in the USA with his sculptures and prints, which never failed to put a smile on the faces of his many viewers. He owned galleries in places like Santa Fe and Key West, home to the rich and famous. His clients included Maria Shriver, Arnold Schwarzenegger, and Sandra Bullock, among others. Some of his sculptures remain on display in the Smithsonian Institute.

Stephen told me a story about Bill Clinton, who, just two weeks after publicly confessing to his affair with Monica Lewinsky, made a surprise visit to Huneck's gallery. Clinton's favourite work was a woodblock print of a dog licking itself, entitled "Because They Can".

Huneck was particularly successful with his books featuring prints of Sally, his beloved black labrador. The first book was called *My Dog's Brain*. It is a charming portrait of what life with a dog consists of: eating, sleeping, scratching, ice cream, love, and much, much more. The children's book *Sally Goes to the Beach* was a *New York Times* bestseller in 2000.

Even at the height of his success, Stephen Huneck still enjoyed nothing more than simply watching his dogs. I found it easy to believe him as he talked earnestly about his four-legged best friends. "If you want to learn anything about generosity of spirit or how to put others before yourself, if you want to know what humour is or to experience pure joy and unconditional love, just look at your dog. My art is simply an expression of the things I learn every day."

I bought Huneck's book *The Dog Chapel* on the way out, and got it signed. When I opened the book that evening, I read this on one of the final pages: "Heaven is where people smile and dogs play." And "You too can build a chapel in memory of your dog, in a place that is always open – your heart."

Huneck believed in the healing power of dogs, nature, art, and love. He hoped to be able to help others through his work. Unfortunately, he was unable to help himself. Dog Mountain fell into financial difficulties: sales and donations no longer brought in enough money to pay his employees, and Stephen and Gwen ultimately had to lay off 90% of their workforce. Huneck was absolutely crushed, and in January 2010 he took his own life. Perhaps he hoped that his death would increase the value of his work and boost revenue. His widow wanted to maintain Dog Mountain in his honour, but she never recovered from the loss of her husband, and she too took her own life three years later.

Dog Mountain is now kept running by the *Friends of Dog Mountain* foundation.[64] Each year they organise dog parties and festivals that attract hundreds of two-legged and four-legged guests.

A chapel that celebrates spiritual connection with our dogs and is open to dogs of all breeds and people of all creeds – could Huneck have left a better legacy?

Dog Mountain and the Dog Chapel are unique places of remembrance. We can all create places like that, but they need not be great works of architecture. When I go out of the kitchen into my garden, I see the red Japanese maple behind the little pond, which I planted on my Lady's grave. Especially since I'd had to leave my first dog at the vet's after he was put down, because I had nowhere to bury him at the time (and pet crematoriums didn't yet exist), I was determined for my old Lady to find her final resting place in the garden that was her home. I was aware that if I sold my house, I'd be leaving the new owner a skeleton in the garden. A friend of mine who moved house twice dug up her dogs each time and reburied them in her new place.

When Lady began to go downhill the autumn before she died, I had a premonition that the end was near. I knew that I had to prepare myself, so I decided – extreme as it may sound – to dig her a grave in the garden. In the event of her death, I wanted to be ready to concentrate entirely on her, without any distractions. I also wanted her to be involved in the decision-making – so one sunny day, I took her into the garden. I let her choose her favourite spot, next to the pond, as she loved water. It had been raining and the ground was soft. I knew that I wouldn't be in the emotional state to dig a grave for her after her death, and I wouldn't be physically capable of it if it happened in winter and the ground had frozen over.

Lady lay down beside me in the sun and watched me as I dug her grave. I think she was pleased with the spot I chose. I dug a hole that met all the legal requirements for animal burials: in my own garden, not in a water conservation area, not on a public road or in a public place, covered by a layer of earth at least 50cm deep. I covered the grave over with boards and shovelled some earth on top. Finally I arranged my collection of exquisite quartz crystals over it. Lady watched me carefully. "So? Do you like it?" I asked her, as I took off my gloves and put away my spade.

"Perfect! But you know you don't actually need that?" She raised her eyebrows.

"Yes, I know, it's just your body. But I'm doing it for my own good, so I know you won't be far away."

"Silly billy. I'll always be with you." She squinted into the sun and stretched out for a nap.

To some people, the idea of digging a grave for a dog before her death might sound heartless, and I admit that I was a little worried it might turn out to be a self-fulfilling prophecy. What if I was "bringing on" her death by digging her grave? But the reality was that my dog was old and the clock was ticking. I didn't have much time left. Everything I could do now would make our goodbyes easier later on.

Many dog owners simply don't want to consider the fact that their young, healthy dog might die at any time. But facing up to the fact that the animals (and people) we love could leave us at any time often leads to the wonderful realisation that we love them even more than we imagined.

In recent years, the ways in which we relive our memories and ritualise remembrance have become more and more diverse. These days you can bury a dog in ways you (still) can't bury people. I buried Lady in my own garden, which will be Shira's resting place one day too. Some people use animal graveyards. One friend of mine had her dog cremated and keeps the urn on her mantelpiece. Another scattered her pet's ashes in all their favourite spots. There are ways of getting your dog's ashes pressed into diamonds that can then be worked into a piece of jewellery – an eternal (and expensive) memento. And some graveyards now allow pets and their owners to be buried in urns together. Depending how much you want to spend on your pet, the possibilities are endless. People who can't give their pet a "proper" burial can use virtual pet graveyards instead, where you send in an epitaph along with your pet's name, date of birth, and date of death. Death announcements can be submitted anonymously or under fake names, and you often come across inscriptions like this one:

You didn't bite, you walked to heel,
You never got depressed.
I can't express the love I feel –
You really were the best.

You thanked me for the things I gave
And always made me smile.
So here's an electronic grave
To send you off in style.

I don't find humorous epitaphs tasteless. On the contrary –
laughter is as natural a part of life as death. When I die, I'd
like people to remember me with a laugh.

What about our dogs? Do they miss us? If they are so firmly
rooted in the here and now, do they still remember us when we
depart this world – and if so, how do they remember us? Do
they think back on times past? On experiences or journeys we
made together, trips to the seaside, or walks in the mountains?
This would be the case if dogs have an "episodic memory" –
a form of recall defined by the ability to remember random
personal experiences and specific events in your own life.
Episodic memory is closely linked to an awareness of the self.
Unlike consciously learning new skills, it means being able to
recall events and experiences arbitrarily – just by virtue of
having been there.

But it's rather tricky to ask dogs how much they remember. To answer this question, the Italian behavioural scientist Claudia Fugazza and her team from the MTA-ELTE Comparative Ethology Research Group in Budapest performed an experiment: they taught 17 dogs a "Do as I do" trick, training them to copy what they saw humans doing.[65]

For example, when a person jumped into the air, the dog imitated them by jumping into the air when they heard the command, "Do it!" This on its own didn't suffice as proof of an episodic memory. It was only proven when the animals were taught to lie down and do nothing else after copying the humans.

After consolidating this exercise, the dogs continued to respond to the command "Do it!" – and surprised the experts by managing to imitate humans when the command was given spontaneously.

In other words, they automatically remembered what they had seen people do, even when they couldn't have known they'd need to remember it.

The scientists concluded that dogs do have an episodic memory, because the animals could still respond to the command "Do it!" a full hour later. Only with time did their memories begin to fade.

Shira, then, has a memory not unlike my own. Big deal! I, along with most dog owners, am pretty surprised such a logical and obvious fact had to be scientifically proven to be believed.

Shira and I went on holiday to an island in the North Sea last year. We used to go there a lot, but eventually stopped visiting. Shira was already craning her neck out of the window as I parked the car behind the dunes. She could already smell the sea. As I lowered the ramp in the boot, I could hardly hold her back: my golden girl bolted off as soon as I gave the word. Old in body, but young in spirit, she hurtled along the narrow path between the dunes, down to the beach and into the sea. Standing in the shallows, she looked back at me, her eyes glowing. "Isn't it great here? Water! Look, water!"

Did she remember our beach holidays of old, or had her labrador instincts simply kicked in when she smelt the sea? Who cares? She was happy, and that was all that mattered to me.

The American writer Mary Carolyn Davies writes, "A good dog never dies. He always stays. He walks besides you on crisp autumn days when frost is on the fields and winter's drawing near. His head is within our hand in his old way."[66]

We don't forget our dogs. And our bodies remember them too: their smell, the sound of their breathing – even their snoring – or the weight of their head resting on our knee. Over the course of our lives together, we developed lots of little rituals, built mutual trust, and became totally secure around one another.

I have been taking photos of Shira throughout her life. I have endless puppy photos, but nowadays I'm taking even more pictures and short videos to remind me of the old Shira. Memories are becoming ever more important.

"All that matters in life are the traces of love we leave behind when we depart," writes Albert Schweitzer.[67] Shira has left so many traces that I will remember her with immense gratitude for the rest of my life.

When we share our lives with dogs, whose lives are so short, and when the time we have left begins to dwindle, we create and rediscover more and more memories every day. Past experiences become more vivid than before, for puppies and people alike. The less time we have left, the more we have to look back on.

May we spend as much time as possible with our old dogs, and fill every day with new memories.

Life
Goes On

"No way! Never! I don't want another dog!" I shouted down the phone to my friend.

She had just told me about a lovely little puppy who would be the perfect match for me. It was only three months since I'd buried Lady. Now seemed like a good moment to take some time out, go travelling, enjoy myself, and do everything I hadn't been able to do before. Above all, though, I never wanted to have to grieve for an animal and suffer like that again.

This was the first of many long phone conversations I had with Corina. A little puppy, a labrador crossbreed, had been born on a tiny island in Denmark. Corina knew the owners and, of course, the puppy's parents. "Lovely dogs. Really cool and relaxed. And the little one... she'd be the dream dog for you!"

"No! And definitely not another puppy. Way too much stress!" Somehow, though, my defences were down. I knew I could trust my friend, an experienced dog trainer, to judge what the "perfect dog" for me would be. But did I really want another one already?

I sat down beside Lady's grave in the garden and thought about it. When is the right time to get a new dog? When are we ready to open our hearts again? I asked myself, "What if I had died and Lady were still alive?" Wouldn't I want her to be happy again and find a new home? Surely the same applied the other way round. Dogs are the personification of unconditional love. They don't want us to be sad. We honour them and their lives by bringing another animal into our homes.

Coping with loss is one of the hardest experiences we go through in our lives. But at some point on our journey we will realise that we never actually owned the creature we're grieving for. And we will see that they'll always be with us in one way or another. We will understand that it is better to have loved and lost a beloved dog than never to have loved at all. Love never dies! If we love another living creature so much that we can grieve for them this deeply, we must have a lot of love within us. And this love cannot be contained – it will continue to reach out and touch others. When a person gives love openly and freely, that person, and ultimately our entire universe, is transformed.

We can never replace a dog we have lost. But we can decide to fill the hole in our lives with fresh love. If we decide to let a new furry friend into our lives, the right one will be out there waiting for us.

When I held Shira, my eight-week-old Danish pup, in my arms for the first time, I knew I had made the right decision. From "I'm never getting another dog" and "absolutely not a puppy", I had come round to "perhaps" and eventually "okay, I'll have a look at her". And then this little bundle of fur tumbled right into my heart. It wasn't until later that my soul became hers, as we began to age together. But in all our time together, I have never regretted my decision for one moment. In my heart of hearts, I knew there was no other path for me to take. No path can skirt around love altogether. Love grows from grief and makes us whole again.

Shira turned 13 this year, and she's doing well. I have just got back from her annual geriatric check, which I always arrange around Easter for sentimental reasons. With a twinkle in one eye and a tear in the other, I take her back to the same vet who put Lady to sleep at Easter all those years ago. That way, I can celebrate Shira and Lady's lives at once. Life and death, happiness and sadness are so tightly interwoven.

At some point in the future, our time together will be over. Until that day, I will continue to enjoy every moment I have with Shira. And when she goes, I will be at her side. I will hold her in my arms, tell her how much I love her, and talk about old times, just as I did with Lady. Then I will grieve, and my heart will break. And one day I will be able to love again.

Old dogs teach us that life is not a problem waiting to be solved, but a sacred secret waiting to be discovered. They show us that they are not just our dogs, but that we are also their humans. They need us, but in reality we need them more. Their zest for life. Their joy. The closer we come to the end, the greater delight we should take in the time we have left. That is the wisest teaching that old dogs leave behind.

What a gift life is. Everything happens exactly as it is meant to happen. Our old dogs are wise to the secret of happiness: give me a bone and I will be happy; give me a place in your heart and *you* will be happy.

Acknowledgements

This book is a very personal letter of love and gratitude to all my four-legged friends who have invited me into their lives and brought me so many wonderful years of happiness and laughter.

In addition, of course, I would also like to thank my two-legged helpers – first and foremost, my agent Uwe Neumahr, from Agence Hoffman in Munich, for all his support. Thank you to Jessica Hein, who commissioned this book, for her faith in me and my ideas. Thank you to the team from Ludwig Verlag – Beatrice Braken-Gülke (media) and Carolin Assmann (events) – for juggling my dates and deadlines. I'm so grateful to you.

Sometimes we find a kindred spirit when we least expect it. My editor Ulrike Strerath-Bolz is one of those people, and it was a real pleasure to work on the manuscript with her.

Thank you to Andrea Weil, my trusty sounding board and personal critic. She achieves the impossible, giving my chaotic first drafts that much-needed polish. I take my hat off to her.

All my dogs have been given a second home by my parents, enjoying "luxury holidays" there while I'm away on book tours or research trips. Thank you. I love you.

My friend Corina, Shira's "godmother", will always have a special place in my heart. She persuaded me to give love a second chance after Lady's death when she placed little Shira in my arms.

And my final thank you goes to all the readers of my *Wolf Magazin* newsletter who opened their hearts to me and told me their stories about their old dogs.

Old dogs are a real blessing. Caring for them and being loved by them is an honour. May we prove ourselves worthy of them.

Author website: www.elli-radinger.de/en

Notes

1   Markus Pössel, "Twins on the road", *Einstein Online*,
    2010, Volume 04, 1008.

2   https://en.wikipedia.org/wiki/Methuselah

3   http://www.bbc.co.uk/newsbeat/article/36080853/
    worlds-oldest-dog-dies-at-30-in-australia-after-going-to-
    sleep-in-her-basket

4   Cornelia Kraus, Samuel Pavard & Daniel Promislow, "The
    Size–Life Span Trade-Off Decomposed: Why Large Dogs
    Die Young", *The American Naturalist*, 2013, Volume 181, Issue
    4, pp. 492-505. 10.1086/669665.

5   https://tandfonline.com/doi/full/10.1080/14649365.2016.1
    274047

6   https://www.pdsa.org.uk/get-involved/our-campaigns/
    pdsa-animal-wellbeing-report/uk-pet-populations-of-dogs-
    cats-and-rabbits

7   https://news.yahoo.com/dogs-snub-people-mean-owners-
    study-053213855.html

8   https://www.thepetcarecard.com/

9   https://www.oldies.org.uk/

10 https://www.pdsa.org.uk/taking-care-of-your-pet/looking-
    after-your-pet/puppies-dogs/the-cost-of-owning-a-dog

11 https://www.maz-online.de/Mehr/Deine-Tierwelt/Geliebte-Haustiere-Das-Geschaeft-mit-der-Tiermedizin

12 https://www.rspca.org.uk/whatwedo/latest/facts

13 https://www1.wdr.de/verbraucher/geld/r-ausgerechnet-geld-ausgeben-100.html

14 Matthew 6:21.

15 Peter F. Cook, Ashley Prichard, Mark Spivak & Gregory S. Berns, "Awake canine fMRI predicts dogs' preference for praise *vs* food", *Social Cognitive and Affective Neuroscience*, Volume 11, Issue 12, 2016, pp. 1853-1862, https://doi.org/10.1093/scan/nsw102

16 https://worldhappiness.report

17 https://www.huffingtonpost.co.uk/entry/worlds-ugliest-dog-2017-martha-mastiff_n_594fa7cce4b05c37bb76f7b3

18 Amanda Jones, *Dog Years: Faithful Friends, Then & Now.* Chronicle Books, 2015.

19 Elli H. Radinger, *The Wisdom of Wolves: How Wolves Can Teach Us To Be More Human.* Penguin UK, 2019.

20 Julia Cameron, *The Artist's Way: A Course in Discovering and Recovering Your Creative Self.* Pan, 1995.

21 https://www.healthline.com/nutrition/cheat-meals

22 Bronnie Ware, *The Top Five Regrets of the Dying: A Life Transformed by the Dearly Departing.* Hay House UK, 2012.

23 Elli H. Radinger, *Minnesota Winter. Eine Liebe in der Wildnis.* Aufbau TB, 2015.

24 https://www.goodreads.com/quotes/2690-i-went-to-the-woods-because-i-wished-to-live

25   https://www.nature.com/articles/s41598-017-12781-x

26   *Underdogs*. Germany, 2007, Director: Jan-Hinrik Drevs.

27   https://nationalpurebreddogday.com/if-you-want-a-friend-in-
washington-get-a-dog/

28   https://gutezitate.com/zitat/213783

29   https://www.aphorismen.de/zitat/12322

30   *Science Advances*, 2017, 10.1126/sciadv.1700398

31   "Dogs Can Discriminate Emotional Expressions of Human
Faces", http://www.cell.com/current-biology/abstract/
S0960-9822(14)01693-5

32   https://www.zeit.de/2006/09/F-Hund

33   https://newsthump.com/2015/04/29/dogs-only-show-
affection-due-to-canine-stockholm-syndrome-finds-study/

34   https://gutezitate.com/zitat/242974

35   https://www.welt.de/kmpkt/article173365538/Darum-sollte-
dein-Hund-oefter-Computerspiele-zocken.html

36   https://www.goodreads.com/quotes/2253-live-as-if-you-
were-to-die-tomorrow-learn-as

37   https://www.jneurosci.org/content/28/28/7031

38   https://www.chaserthebordercollie.com/

39   Carl Naughton, *Neugier: So schaffen Sie Lust auf Neues
und Veränderung*. Econ Verlag, 2016.

40   http://www.spiegel.de/wissenschaft/natur/hunde-verstehen-
inhalt-und-tonfall-einer-aussage-a-1110161.html

41   https://time.com/103396/we-trust-strangers-even-when-it-
doesnt-make-sense-to-do-so/

42   https://www.smava.de/presse/pressemitteilungen/jeder-zweite-wuerde-crowdfunding-projekte-mitfinanzieren/

43   https://gutezitate.com/zitat/118540

44   Margareta Magnusson, *The Gentle Art of Swedish Death Cleaning: How to Free Yourself and Your Family from a Lifetime of Clutter*. Canongate, 2017.

45   https://www.brainyquote.com/quotes/will_rogers_167212

46   *PLOS ONE*, 2014; https://l.org/doi 10.1371/journal.pone.0107794

47   https://www.presseportal.de/pm/54882/3819665

48   Detlef Singer & Jean C Roché, *Vögel Mitteleuropas und ihre Stimmen*. Frackh-Kosmos, 1998.

49   "Animal Cognition: Empathic-like responding by domestic dogs (Canis familiaris) to distress in humans: an exploratory study", https://link.springer.com/article/10.1007/s10071-012-0510-1

50   https://www.galileo.tv/earth-nature/schau-mir-die-augen-darum-koennen-wir-dem-hundeblick-nicht-widerstehen/

51   http://booksandjournals.brillonline.com/content/journals/10.1163/15685306-12341440

52   http://www.dailygood.org/story/28/emotional-lives-of-animals-marc-bekoff/

53   https://en.wikipedia.org/wiki/Serenity_Prayer

54   http://www.independent.co.uk/news/world/europe/dog-russia-stays-with-injured-friend-railway-tracks-panda-lucy-video-watch-a7497551.html

55   Elli H. Radinger, *The Wisdom of Wolves: How Wolves Can Teach Us To Be More Human*. Penguin UK, 2019.

56   https://notsuredamus.wordpress.com/2011/04/19/delta-
     hero-dog-of-pompeii/

57   Isaiah Spiegel, *A Ghetto Dog*, in: Irving Howe, Ben Shahn &
     Eliezer Greenberg (ed.), *A Treasury of Yiddish Stories*. Andre
     Deutsch, 1955. You can listen to the heart-wrenching full story
     here: https://youtube.com/watch?v=x7MQkvsQCh4

58   The Torah instructs Jewish people to wear tefillin during
     weekly morning prayers. It binds the head, heart and hands,
     and is supposed to ensure that thoughts, feelings and actions
     work together. http://www.judentum-projekt.de/religion/
     religioesegrundlagen/gebetskleidung/

59   Sigmund Freud, *Zeitgemäßes über Krieg und Tod*, Gesammelte
     Werke 10, London 1946, p. 341.

60   https://www.wn.de/Welt/Kultur/2013/04/Kabarettist-
     Jochen-Busse-in-Muensters-Aula-am-Aasee-Der-Tod-sucht-
     schon-einen-Parkplatz

61   Sogyal Rinpoche, *The Tibetan Book of Living and Dying*. Rider, 2008.

62   Elisabeth Kübler Ross & David Kessler, *Life Lessons: How Our Mortality
     Can Teach Us About Life And Living*. Simon & Schuster UK, 2001.

63   https://www.snopes.com/glurge/abbey.asp

64   https://www.dogmt.com/

65   https://www.wissenschaft.de/umwelt-natur/woran-sich-
     hunde-erinnern/

66   https://www.dogquotations.com/dog-quotes-author-d.html

67   https://www.zitate-online.de/literaturzitate/aphorismen/

Elli with her dog, Shira, aged 13

Elli H. Radinger (author) is an international bestselling author specialising in wolves and dogs. She has written numerous books about her wolf research in Yellowstone National Park, and gives frequent lectures and readings. She put her wolf research on hold in order to help her 13-year-old dog Shira through the final years of her life. "Shira is family, so she takes priority. That's the number one lesson I learned from wolves."

George Robarts (translator) studied German and Italian at Oxford University, where he specialised in prose and verse translation, graduating with a First. He works in publishing in London.

Picture Index

Every reasonable effort has been made to contact all copyright holders, but if there are any errors or omissions, we will insert the appropriate acknowledgement in subsequent printings of the book.